PRAYERS
THAT CHANGE THINGS

PRAY GOD'S WORD—GET HIS ANSWERS

Lloyd Hildebrand

PRAYERS
THAT CHANGE THINGS

PRAY GOD'S WORD—GET HIS ANSWERS

Lloyd Hildebrand

BRIDGE
LOGOS
FOUNDATION

Alachua, Florida 32615

Bridge-Logos
Alachua, FL 32615 USA

Prayers That Change Things
by Lloyd Hildebrand

Printed in the United States of America.

Library of Congress Catalog Card Number:
    2011945353
International Standard Book Number
    978-1-61036-105-7

Unless otherwise noted, all Scripture quotations are from the King James Version of the Holy Bible.

DEDICATION

To Harold and Beverlee Chadwick, who have prayed daily for Bridge-Logos and have worked faithfully in this ministry for many years. You are true prayer warriors.

Thank you for your prayers, Bev and Hal, and thank you, Bev, for editing this book so carefully.

May God richly bless you both in every possible way as you continue to serve Him in so many ways. We have all learned so much from you.

CONTENTS

Chapter One: Pray God's Word—
Get His Answers 11

Chapter Two: Meditate Upon the Scriptures
As You Pray 17

Chapter Three:
Praying God's Promises Into Existence 31

Chapter Four: Word-Prayers About
Your Feelings and Conditions 39

1. Addictions/Obsessions 45
2. Anger/Wrath 49
3. Anxiety and Stress 53
4. Bitterness 57
5. Boredom 61
6. Brokenheartedness 65
7. Burnout 69
8. Conceit 73
9. Confusion 77
10. Defensiveness 81
11. Discontentedness 83
12. Discouragement 87
13. Dismay 91
14. Doubt 95
15. Envy 97
16. Fatigue 101
17. Fear 103

18. Gluttony/Overeating 105
19. Gossiping 109
20. Helplessness 113
21. Hopelessness 115
22. Inconsistency 119
23. Indecisiveness 123
24. Indifference 127
25. Irritability 131
26. Laziness 135
27. Loneliness 139
28. Lying 143
29. Moodiness 147
30. Mourning/Grief 151
31. Negativity 155
32. Nervousness 159
33. Passivity 163
34. Perfectionism 167
35. Pessimism 171
36. Regretfulness 175
37. Rejection 179
38. Sadness/Depression............................. 183
39. Self-centeredness 185
40. Self-consciousness 189
41. Self-destructiveness............................. 193
42. Self-righteousness...............................197
43. Sensitivity 201
44. Sexism 205
45. Shame 209
46. Short-sightedness 213
47. Sinfulness..217

48. Skepticism 221
49. Suicidal Tendencies 225
50. Talkativeness 229
51. Temper 233
52. Trials 237
53. Unthankfulness 241
54. Weakness 245
Chapter Five:
Prayer Promises From God's Word 249

CHAPTER ONE

PRAY GOD'S WORD
GET HIS ANSWERS

*Your word is a lamp to my feet
and a light to my path.*

(Psalm 119:105, AMP)

God's Word presents God's complete will for you. It is filled with His promises to you. This is why it is imperative for you to:

- Read God's Word
- Understand God's Word
- Memorize God's Word
- Meditate upon God's Word
- Stand upon God's Word
- Trust God's Word
- Love God's Word
- Receive God's Word
- Believe God's Word
- Pray God's Word

This book is about all these important actions, but its primary focus is upon learning to pray God's Word.

Why It Is Important to Pray God's Word

Why is it important for you to pray God's Word? Doing so results in several personal benefits:

- Your faith will increase, and this will enable you to receive even more of God's promises.

- Your mind will be renewed, and this will cause you to see everything differently.

- You will know God's perfect will.

- You will be able to walk in the truth.

- You will grow in the nurture and admonition of the Lord.

- You will draw very close to God and have intimate fellowship with Him.

- You will learn God's ways and they will become yours.

- You will understand God's answers to your prayers.

- Your outlook will change.

- You will change in positive ways.

- You will behold the Lamb of God, who is the very center of the Bible.

Personalizing the Prayers of the Psalms

To start, let me encourage you to personalize the following biblical prayers about God's Word (from Psalms 118 and 119) and apply them to your own life. This is a great way to learn how to pray the Scriptures:

"Open to me the gates of righteousness; I will go through them, and I will praise the LORD" (Psalm 118:19, NKJV).

"Deal bountifully with Your servant, that I may live and keep Your word" (Psalm 119:17, NKJV).

"Open my eyes that I may see wondrous things from Your law" (Psalm 119:18, NKJV).

"Teach me Your statutes, make me understand the way of Your precepts; so shall I meditate on Your wonderful works" (Psalm 119:26-27, NKJV).

"Strengthen me according to Your word" (Psalm 119:28, NKJV).

"Oh, how I love Your law! It is my meditation all the day. You, through Your commandments, make me wiser than my enemies; for they are ever with me" (Psalm 119:97-99, NKJV).

"For I will keep the commandments of my God! Uphold me according to Your word, that I may live; and do not let me be ashamed of my hope" (Psalm 119:115-117, NKJV).

"Give me understanding, and I shall live" (Psalm 119:144, NKJV).

These are just a few of the personal prayers related to God's Word that are found in Psalm 119 (and throughout the Psalms). They reveal so many things about the power of the Word of God. Notice that:

- It is a source of strength for your life.
- Understanding God's Word provides you with so many things.
- It gives you wisdom.
- It is a true eye-opener.
- God's Word should be a focal point for your life.

Prayer Changes Things

For these reasons and so many others you must learn to pray God's Word. The expression, "Prayer changes things," takes on new meaning when you do so. Indeed, these prayers really change things. Most importantly, they change *you* and the way you look at things in your life.

The prayers in this book are built directly from the Bible. They are life-imparting, life-generating, life-giving, and life-sustaining prayers. Pray them from your heart; then listen for God to speak to you. He is always speaking through His Word, and He sometimes speaks in that still, small voice deep within your spirit.

As you learn to pray this way, remember these important words: "All Scripture is given by inspiration of God, and is profitable for doctrine, for reproof, for correction, for instruction in righteousness, that the man of God may be complete, thoroughly equipped for every good work" (2 Timothy 3:16-17, NKJV). It is also profitable for prayer and meditation, as you will now see.

"More things are wrought by prayer than this world dreams of..." (Alfred, Lord Tennyson).

CHAPTER TWO

MEDITATE UPON THE SCRIPTURES
AS YOU PRAY

This Book of the Law [the Bible] shall not depart from your mouth, but you shall meditate in it day and night, that you may observe to do according to all that is written in it.

For then you will make your way prosperous, and then you will have good success.

(Joshua 1:8, NKJV)

Andrew Murray wrote, "It is in meditation that the heart holds and appropriates the Word. . . .The intellect gathers and prepares the food upon which we are to feed. In meditation the heart takes it and feeds upon it."

Meditation is such an important activity for Christians to engage in, because it results in so many blessings in our lives. It is a source of peace and strength.

As you pray the Scriptures, take time to meditate upon them. This will lead you to walk in the paths of righteousness, grant you spiritual prosperity, and lead you to success in all that you do.

Take Time to Pause and Calmly Think About the Words of God

Throughout the Psalms we see the word *Selah* appearing frequently. This Hebrew word means, "Pause, and calmly think of that."

This is a good direction to remember while we are praying the Scriptures. Take time to pause and chew on the words you are reading and praying, reflect on them, and let them become a part of you. It would be good to remember to apply "Selah" after you read any verse or passage of the Bible.

Meditation is a peaceful way to ponder God's Word. It builds confidence and stability into our lives, peace within our spirits, and a positive outlook in all that we do. It keeps us calm and helps us to experience God's rest in all we do.

"Be still, and know that I am God" (Psalm 46:10).

Bible Memorization

David asked, "Wherewithal shall a young man cleanse his way? By taking heed thereto according to thy word. With my whole heart have I sought thee: O let me not wander from thy commandments. Thy word have I hid in my heart, that I might not sin against thee" (Psalm 119:9-11).

This passage speaks of Bible memorization, which is an important part of praying the Word and meditating upon its precepts. As we hide God's Word in our hearts through memorization, we are able to call it forth whenever we need to pray or participate in spiritual warfare, as Jesus did. (See Luke 4.)

Bible meditation helps us to learn to focus our thoughts on what is important, as Jesus told us to do: "But seek ye first the kingdom of God, and his righteousness; and all these things shall be added unto you" (Matthew 6:33).

Meditation, then, involves focusing, pondering, reflecting upon, contemplation, and even planning. It is a sure-fire method that God has put in place for us. He wants us to learn to pray the Scriptures and meditate upon them because these habits will help us to experience everything He has for us.

"Finally, brethren, whatsoever things are true, whatsoever things are honest, whatsoever things are just, whatsoever things are pure, whatsoever things are lovely, whatsoever things are of good report; if there be any virtue, and if there be any praise, think on these things" (Philippians 4:8). God's Word is filled with things

19

that are true, honest, just, pure, lovely, and of good report.

What Happens When We Learn to Meditate?

Here's another Bible verse about the importance of meditation: "Blessed is the man who walks not in the counsel of the ungodly, nor stands in the path of sinners, nor sits in the seat of the scornful; but his delight is in the law of the LORD, and in His law he *meditates* day and night. He shall be like a tree planted by the rivers of water, that brings forth its fruit in its season, whose leaf also shall not wither; and whatever he does shall prosper" (Psalm 1:1-3, NKJV, italics mine).

Bible meditation leads to contemplation, which is thoughtful study and inspection of what is before us. A subtle distinction between biblical meditation and biblical contemplation was given by Dr. Brian Allison: "What is Biblical meditation? What is Biblical contemplation? Though a close relationship exists between these two activities, there is a subtle distinction between them. Biblical meditation is the act or activity of pondering, of mentally chewing over, *the revealed will and ways of God/Christ*. It is the sustained reflection on disclosed truth....Biblical contemplation is the activity of focusing on, of being mentally absorbed or preoccupied with *the revealed person of God/Christ*. It is inwardly beholding or gazing upon God."

As we meditate upon Bible truths through prayer, we are able to contemplate or behold the beauty of God, as David describes in the Psalms: "One thing I have desired of the LORD, that will I seek: that I may dwell in the house of the LORD all the days of my life, to behold the beauty of the LORD, and to inquire in His temple" (Psalm 27:4, NKJV).

Therefore, as you can readily see, praying the Scriptures and meditation on their truths leads us into greater intimacy with God—contemplating about who He is and beholding Him.

Chewing on God's Word

Merrill F. Unger wrote, "Meditation upon God's Word is fast becoming a lost art among many Christian people. This holy exercise of pondering over the Word, chewing it as an animal chews its cud to get its sweetness and nutritive virtue into the heart and life, takes time, which ill fits into the speed of our modern age. Today most Christians' devotions are too hurried, and their lives too rushed." (Taken from *Pathways to Power* by Merrill F. Unger.)

The word "meditation" comes from the word we use to describe the process of chewing the cud (mastication) that a ruminant does. In fact, rumination is another word for meditation. A cow, for example, chews its cud, swallows it, brings it up again, chews it again, and swallows it again. We must do the same as we meditate upon a Bible passage. Chew it, swallow it, bring it up again, etc. This is the process of rumination and meditation upon the Word.

Unger's words are certainly true. It would behoove us to follow the encouragement of the Prophet Isaiah who wrote, "In returning and rest you shall be saved; in quietness and confidence shall be your strength" (Isaiah 30:15, NKJV).

George Mueller and Meditation

A great man of faith, George Mueller, wrote the following entry in his journal, dated May 9, 1841: "It has pleased the Lord to teach me a truth, the benefit of which I have not lost for more than fourteen years. The point is this: I saw more clearly than ever that the first great primary business to which I ought to attend every day was, to have my soul happy in the Lord. . . . not how much I might serve the Lord. . . .but how I might get my soul into a happy state, and how my inner man might be nourished.

"For I might seek to set the truth before the unconverted, I might seek to benefit believers... and yet, not being happy in the Lord, and not being nourished and strengthened in my inner man day by day, all this might not be attended to in a right spirit. Before this time my practice had been...to give myself to prayer after having dressed myself in the morning.

"Now, I saw that the most important thing I had to do was to give myself to the reading of the Word of God, *and to meditation on it*, that thus my heart might be comforted, encouraged, warned, reproved, instructed; and that this, by means of the Word of God, *whilst meditating on it*, my heart might be brought into experimental communion with the Lord" (italics mine).

Notice all that George Mueller learned through Bible meditation. As a result, for more than four decades he was able to care for his orphans and participate in other ministries without ever having to make an appeal for funds.

Bible meditation enabled him to learn to walk by faith, not by sight, and to experience success and prosperity in all his endeavors. It will do the same for you.

The Sweetness of Meditation

Meditation is sweet to God, as David points out: "I will sing to the LORD as long as I live; I will sing praise to my God while I have my being. *May my meditation be sweet to Him*; I will be glad in the LORD" (Psalm 104:33-34, NKJV, italics mine).

David learned what Jeremy Taylor tells us: "Meditation is the tongue of the soul and the language of our spirit."

Meditation enabled David's confidence to grow: "Because Your lovingkindness is better than life,

23

my lips shall praise You, thus I will bless you while I live; I will lift up my hands in Your name. My soul shall be satisfied as with marrow and fatness, and my mouth shall praise You with joyful lips. *When I remember You on my bed, I meditate on You in the night watches*, because You have been my help, therefore in the shadow of Your wings I will rejoice. My soul follows close behind You; Your right hand upholds me" (Psalm 63:3-8, NKJV, italics mine).

Bible Truths About Meditation and Its Benefits

Let us look at other truths about Bible meditation that were freely expressed in the Psalms:

"I will remember the works of the LORD: surely I will remember thy wonders of old. I will meditate also of all thy work, and talk of thy doings" (Psalm 77:11-12). Meditation upon the Word of God leads us to share His truths with others, to witness to His power, and to remind others of all God has done.

"I have rejoiced in the way of thy testimonies, as much as in all riches. I will meditate in thy precepts, and have respect unto thy ways. I will delight myself in thy statutes: I will not forget thy word" (Psalm 119:14-16). The words "testimonies," "the Law," "statutes," "Word," "precepts," "commands," "ways," and "commandments" may be viewed as being synonymous with the Bible. I love how the Psalmist takes delight in God's Word, and He rejoices in the testimonies of the Lord. We must do the same, and the more we get into the Word through prayer and meditation, the more joyful we will be.

"And I will delight myself in thy commandments, which I have loved. My hands also will I lift up unto thy commandments, which I have loved; and I will meditate in thy statutes" (Psalm 119:47-48). Notice how the Psalmist loved the commandments of God and took great delight in them. This is a good goal for each of us to strive for. It is clear that meditating on the words of the Bible will make this possible for us.

It is fitting to conclude this section by meditating on Psalm 19:14 and making it our prayer: "Let the words of my mouth, and the meditation of my heart, be acceptable in thy sight, O Lord, my strength, and my redeemer." Amen—so be it. David prayed this prayer, and so must we.

Peace Like a River

The Aaronic Blessing says, "The Lord bless you and keep you; the Lord make His face shine upon you, and be gracious to you; the Lord lift up His countenance upon you, and give you peace" (Numbers 6:24-26, NKJV).

Bible meditation is bathed in peace. Thomas á Kempis wrote, "If you wish to grow in your spiritual life, you must not allow yourself to be caught up in the workings of the world; you must find time alone, away from the noise and confusion, from the allure of power and wealth." Such a place is the best place for meditation.

"Be careful for nothing; but in everything by prayer and supplication with thanksgiving let your requests be make known unto God. And the peace of God, which passeth all understanding, shall keep your hearts and minds through Christ Jesus" (Philippians 4:6-7).

This is peace like a river, a river that flows through Bible meditation and prayer.

Focal Points of Meditation

When we pray the Scriptures and meditate upon them, several focal points for us to concentrate upon will come to mind, and we can meditate upon each of these as we pray:

The multiple blessings of God. David wrote, "Bless the LORD, O my soul; and all that is within me, bless His holy name! Bless the LORD, O my soul, and forget not all His benefits" (Psalm 103:1-2, NKJV). Meditation leads to a thankful heart.

God—our Abba-Father. God is the focal point of our meditation. He is our everlasting Father, the Father of lights with whom there is no variableness or shadow of turning. (See James 1:17.) David wrote, "When I remember You on my bed, I meditate on You in the night watches" (Psalm 63:6, NKJV). There is a place of quiet rest near to the heart of God.

The Word of God. As we pray the Word, we learn to meditate upon it, as the Psalmist declared, "Oh, how I love Your law! It is my meditation all the day" (Psalm 119:97, NKJV). God's Word is a smorgasbord of truth for us to feast upon.

The Unfailing Love of God. God's loving-kindness is better than life, and it is good to meditate upon His great and steadfast love. Psalm 48:9 says: "We have thought of thy lovingkindness, O God, in the midst of thy temple." God is love, and His love is better than life to us. Meditation helps us to experience His love in all its fullness.

There are so many other appropriate focal points for meditation, such as God's power, the truth of God's Word, His works, His majesty and glory, His name, the blood of Jesus, the powerful promises of God, His creation, His justice, His mercy, and His grace. Incorporate these into your moments of meditation.

"Turn your eyes upon Jesus. Look full in His wonderful face, and the things of Earth will grow strangely dim in the light of His glory and grace."

Results of Bible Meditation

There is great power in God's Word, and Bible meditation enables you to gain access to that power. "For the word of God is quick, and powerful, and sharper than any twoedged sword, piercing even to the dividing asunder of soul and spirit, and of the joints and marrow, and is a discerner of the thoughts and intents of the heart" (Hebrews 4:12).

Here are some other things that Bible meditation will bring into your life:

- It will draw you closer to God.
- It will remind you of who God is and what He has done for you.
- It cultivates love for God and His Word.
- It enables you to appropriate and experience the love of God.
- It gives you fresh insights and spiritual understanding.
- It is a source of comfort and strength.
- It empowers you to be a true witness for Jesus Christ.
- It fosters praise and worship.
- It brings joy to your heart.
- It enables you to receive all God's promises.
- It brings answers to your prayers.
- It changes you in unexpected ways.

- It renews your mind.
- It cleanses you.
- It restores your soul.
- It enables you to trust the Lord with all your heart.
- It quickens your spirit.
- It produces fruit.
- It leads you into new realms of victory and success.
- It blesses you.
- It helps you to understand God, others, and yourself.

Murie Lester wrote, "Silent in God's presence, you can relax yourself completely."

Isaiah wrote, "In quietness and in confidence shall be your strength" (Isaiah 30:15).

As you can see, Bible meditation is a very important activity to engage in on a daily basis, for it brings about so many wonderful things in our lives.

My prayer for you is that God, ". . . the Father of glory, may give unto you the spirit of wisdom and revelation in the knowledge of him: the eyes of your understanding being enlightened; that ye may know what is the hope of his calling, and what are the riches of the glory of his inheritance in the saints, and what is the exceeding greatness of his power to us-ward who believe, according to the working of His mighty power . . ." (Ephesians 1:17-19).

CHAPTER THREE

PRAYING GOD'S PROMISES INTO EXISTENCE

There are more than 3000 promises in the Word of God, and it is exceedingly important to realize that each of these is a personal promise from the Father to you. You can stand upon His promises, believe His promises, receive His promises, trust His promises, claim His promises, and expect His promises to come into existence in your life.

Let's review just a few of His promises here:

- "Wait on the LORD; be of good courage, and he shall strengthen thine heart: wait, I say, on the LORD" (Psalm 27:14). God promises to strengthen your heart as you learn to wait upon Him through prayer, meditation, and worship.

- "O fear the LORD, ye his saints: for there is no want to them that fear him" (Psalm 34:9). As we learn to fear (reverence, respect, and honor) the Lord, He will supply all our needs.

- "Delight thyself also in the LORD; and he shall give thee the desires of thine heart. Commit thy way unto the LORD; trust also in him; and he shall bring it to pass" (Psalm 37:4-5). God promises to give you the desires of your heart if you will learn to commit your way unto Him and trust in Him.

- "God is our refuge and strength, a very present help in trouble" (Psalm 46:1). This is a simple statement of fact that is God's promise to us. He will be our refuge, our strength, and a very present help in trouble.

- "But they that wait upon the LORD shall renew their strength; they shall mount up with wings as eagles: they shall run, and not be weary; and they shall walk, and not faint" (Isaiah 40:31). God says that your strength will be renewed and your weariness will depart if you wait upon Him.

Have you noticed that many of God's promises are conditional in that they can only be received if we do our part in the wonderful relationship we have with our heavenly Father? God will bless us with His promises if we will learn to wait upon Him, fear Him, have courage, and take our delight in Him.

Walking with God is walking upon His promises, for they are stepping stones to all the good things

God has in store for us. Good relationships in life require a commitment, open communication, trust, respect, and giving and receiving. Our relationship with God is just the same. Notice the words of this promise, which is one of my favorite verses of Scripture: "Trust in the LORD with all thine heart; and lean not unto thine own understanding. In all thy ways acknowledge him, and he shall direct thy paths" (Proverbs 3:5-6).

What Does God Promise to You?

Teaching and Guidance. "I will instruct thee and teach thee in the way which thou shalt go: I will guide thee with mine eye" (Psalm 32:8).

Deliverance. "And call upon me in the day of trouble: I will deliver thee, and thou shalt glorify me" (Psalm 50:15).

Strength. "Fear thou not; for I am with thee: be not dismayed; for I am thy God: I will strengthen thee; yea, I will help thee; yea, I will uphold thee with the right hand of my righteousness" (Isaiah 41:10).

Personal Help. "For I the LORD thy God will hold thy right hand, saying unto thee, Fear not; I will help thee" (Isaiah 41:13).

Answered Prayer and Revelation. "Call unto me, and I will answer thee, and shew thee great and mighty things, which thou knowest not" (Jeremiah 33:3).

Spiritual Sustenance and Rest. "I will feed my flock, and I will cause them to lie down, saith the Lord GOD" (Ezekiel 34:15).

Showers of Blessing. "And I will make them and the places round about my hill a blessing; and I will cause the shower to come down in his season; there shall be showers of blessing" (Ezekiel 34:26).

Healing and Love. "I will heal their backsliding, I will love them freely: for mine anger is turned away from him" (Hosea 14:4).

Rest. "Come unto me, all ye that labour and are heavy laden, and I will give you rest. Take my yoke upon you, and learn of me; for I am meek and lowly in heart: and ye shall find rest unto your souls" (Matthew 11:28-29).

Forgiveness. "And when you stand praying, forgive, if ye have ought against any: that your Father also which is in heaven may forgive you your trespasses" (Mark 11:25).

Provision. "Give, and it shall be given unto you; good measure, pressed down, and shaken together, and running over, shall men give into your bosom. For with the same measure that ye mete withal it shall be measured to you again" (Luke 6:38).

Everlasting Life. "He that heareth my word, and believeth on him that sent me, hath everlasting life, and shall not come into condemnation; but is passed from death unto life" (John 5:24).

Greater Works. "He that believeth on me, the works that I do shall he do also; and greater works than these shall he do; because I go unto my Father. And whatsoever ye shall ask in my name, that will I do, that the Father may be glorified in the Son. If ye shall ask any thing in my name, I will do it" (John 14:12-14).

Comfort. "I will not leave you comfortless: I will come to you" (John 14:18).

Peace. "Peace I leave with you, my peace I give unto you: not as the world giveth, give I unto you. Let not your heart be troubled, neither let it be afraid" (John 14:27).

Spiritual Knowledge. "Howbeit when he, the Spirit of truth, is come, he will guide you into all truth: for he shall not speak of himself; but whatsoever he shall hear, that shall he speak: and he will shew you things to come" (John 16:13).

Power. "But ye shall receive power, after that the Holy Ghost is come upon you: and ye shall be witnesses unto me both in Jerusalem, and in all Judaea, and in Samaria, and unto the uttermost part of the earth" (Acts 1:8).

As I've gone through the list above, I've been overwhelmed with all that God promises to us, and these are but a few of His personal promises to us. It's simply amazing to know how much He loves us and wants to bless us.

In reality, He has already blessed us in so many ways, as Paul points out: "Blessed be the God and Father of our Lord Jesus Christ, who hath blessed us with all spiritual blessings in heavenly places in Christ" (Ephesians 1:3).

The appropriate response to this these realities of our faith is Hallelujah! Praise the Lord! Wow!

It is important to realize that God's promises are not magical formulas. In order to pray God's promises into existence into our lives, we must be sure that we are doing what God expects of us. Here are some of the prerequisites that God has put in place for us to follow in order to receive His promises and His answers to our prayers:

Faith. "But without faith it is impossible to please him: for he that cometh to God must believe that he is, and that he is a rewarder of them that diligently seek him" (Hebrews 11:6).

Fear of God. "The angel of the LORD encampeth round about them that fear him, and delivereth them" (Psalm 34:7).

Seeking the Lord. "Ask, and it shall be given you; seek, and ye shall find; knock, and it shall be opened unto you: for every one that asketh receiveth and he that seeketh findeth; and to him that knocketh it shall be opened" (Matthew 7:7-8).

Righteousness. "But seek ye first the kingdom of God, and his righteousness; and all these things shall be added unto you" (Matthew 6:33).

Waiting on the Lord. "Rest in the LORD, and wait patiently for him" (Psalm 37:7).

Commitment. "Keep that which is committed to thy trust, avoiding profane and vain babblings, and oppositions of science falsely so called" (1 Timothy 6:20).

Trust. "Unto thee, O LORD, do I lift up my soul. O my God, I trust in thee: let me not be ashamed" (Psalm 25:1-2).

A Contrite Spirit. "The LORD is nigh unto them that are of a broken heart; and saveth such as be of a contrite spirit" (Psalm 34:18).

Abiding in Christ. "If ye abide in me, and my words abide in you, ye shall ask what ye will, and it shall be done unto you" (John 15:7).

CHAPTER FOUR

WORD-PRAYERS ABOUT YOUR FEELINGS AND CONDITIONS

These are some of the things we must do in order to pray God's promises into existence into our lives. In effect, they are all components of our relationship with the Lord, which is the key ingredient in getting answers to our prayers.

We must stay close to Him and seek Him at all times with all our hearts. As we do so, His promises will be fulfilled in our lives and so many good things will happen to us.

Even in the bad times, His promises will be at work. David wrote, "Yea though I walk through the valley of the shadow of death, I will fear no evil: for thou art with me; thy rod and thy staff they comfort me" (Psalm 23:4).

According to one count, there are 3,573 promises in the Bible—more than ten for each day of the year. Yes, you can pray these promises into existence as you grow in the grace and knowledge of the Lord. As you do so, remember these important words:

"Whereby are given unto us exceeding great and precious promises: that by these ye might be partakers of the divine nature, having escaped the corruption that is in the world through lust" (2 Peter 1:4).

"For all the promises of God in him are yes and in him Amen, unto the glory of God by us" (2 Corinthians 1:20).

"That ye be not slothful, but followers of them who through faith and patience inherit the promises" (Hebrews 6:12).

"Who through faith subdued kingdoms, wrought righteousness, obtained promises, stopped the mouth of lions, quenched the violence of fire, escaped the edge of the sword, out of weakness were made strong, waxed valiant in fight, turned to flight the armies of the aliens" (Hebrews 11:33-34).

All these promises are yours! You are an overcomer through God's precious promises. He has blessed you with every spiritual blessing, and He wants you to experience those blessings every day. Take a look at this promise: "He who overcomes shall inherit all things, and I will be his God and he shall be my son" (Revelation 21:7, NKJV).

The promises are a part of that divine inheritance—a true treasure that your Father has bequeathed to you. Each one is stamped with His love and His great desire for you to receive everything He has in store for you.

Your feelings reside within the part of you that is known as your soul. God is in the soul-restoring business, and He wants to help you with your emotions. David prayed, "Restore unto me the joy of thy salvation; and uphold me with thy free spirit" (Psalm 51:12).

God wants you to experience His joy—a deep and abiding joy that is not based upon the circumstances of your life. Peter J. Kreeft writes, "Joy seems to have a necessity to it, as God does. God not only is but could not be otherwise, could not change. We change, so we are not always in joy, nor joy in us; but joy itself is unchangeable, eternal, and necessary. When it comes, though it appears new to us, a surprise, it seems old, ancient, having existed 'before the beginning of time.'. . . Pleasure and happiness have nothing of that air of eternity about them that joy does. . . .

"Yet the joy in our spirit does not stay there, bottled up and stagnant. Spirit is essentially dynamic, and its joy flows out in three directions:

back to God in gratitude and rejoicing, out to others like a watering fountain, and into our own soul and body as a sort of overspill. Joyful feelings and thoughts, even pleasure and health, result from joy; and this is a foretaste of heaven."

As you pray the prayers in this section of the book, I hope you will enjoy a foretaste of Heaven, where you will find fullness of joy and pleasures forevermore. (See Psalm 16:11.) God will not take His joy from you. It is always within you and you can find it if you look deep within. May the wellsprings of His joy overflow from your spirit and fill your soul with gladness.

"Joy is like a well containing sweet water. It is not enough to know the water is there or even to drill the well. If the well is to be useful, the water must be brought to the surface. Those who know Christ have found the source of joy" (Charles R. Hembree).

Grace brings joy to us. "See this Kingdom of God is now found within us. The grace of the Holy Spirit shines forth and warms us, and, overflowing with many and varied scents into the air around us, regales our senses with heavenly delight, as it fills our hearts with joy inexpressible" (St. Seraphim of Sarov).

This is healing of your emotions; this is perfect peace and spiritual strength. Remember, "The joy of the LORD is your strength" (Nehemiah 8:10), so when you are feeling downcast, even in times of grief and loss, God's joy is still there. I believe the Word-prayers in this section of the book will help you experience the joy of the Lord in all its fullness.

The prayers are arranged in alphabetical order to enable you to locate them more readily. The Scripture references are listed after each prayer, and a personal affirmation of faith is stated for you to take your stand upon.

1

✦

ADDICTIONS/ OBSESSIONS

Stand fast therefore in the liberty

wherewith Christ hath made us free,

and be not entangled again

with the yoke of bondage.

(Galatians 5:1)

Central Focus: God wants you to be free from all addictions and addictive tendencies, and His truth will make you free. (See John 3:32.)

Prayer: Father God, I thank you for showing me that the addiction that has been holding me hostage for so long is a form of idolatry. Help me not to be given over to any form of addiction or idolatry any longer. Instead, I want to seek first your kingdom and your righteousness; then I know you will add all things to me. I renounce this addiction to _____ and all forms of idolatry in my life.

With your help and through your grace, I will stand fast in the liberty wherewith Christ has made me free, and I will not be entangled with this yoke of bondage any longer. Thank you, Lord, for freeing me. It is wonderful to know that I've entered into the glorious liberty you have provided for me.

Help me to be led by your Spirit at all times, Lord. Keep me from idolatry in all its forms. Fill me with your Holy Spirit, that I would bear His fruit in my life at all times—love, joy, peace, longsuffering, gentleness, goodness, faith, meekness, and temperance (or self-control). Help me to walk in the Spirit, that I would not ever fulfill the lusts of my flesh.

With your help, Father, I will rule over my spirit at all times, because I know that a person who has no control over his spirit is like a city that is broken down and without walls. Set me free from all addictions, Father. I love you. Your power is at work within me.

As I confess my sins to you, I know you are forgiving me and cleansing me from all unrighteousness. It feels so wonderful to me to be able to enter into the glorious liberty of your children, Father. Now I know without any shadow of doubt that nothing will ever be able to separate me from your love which is in Christ Jesus, my Lord.

Indeed, I am more than a conqueror through Him! Thank you, Father.

Scriptures: Matthew 6:33; Galatians 5:18; Galatians 5:1; Romans 8:21; Galatians 5:19-21; Galatians 5:22-23; Galatians 5:16; Proverbs 25:28; 1 John 1:9; Romans 8:29; Romans 8:37.

Personal Affirmation: I am no longer an addict, and I will not permit myself to be in bondage to any form of idolatry anymore.

Reflection: *"The God who gave us life, gave us liberty at the same time"* (Thomas Jefferson).

2

❧

ANGER/WRATH

Let all bitterness, and wrath, and anger,

and clamour, and evil speaking, be put away from you, with all malice.
And be ye kind one to another, tenderhearted, forgiving one another, even as God for Christ's sake hath forgiven you.

(Ephesians 4:31-32)

Central Focus: Anger never works righteousness in my life. Anger and wrath are destructive forces. God will help me to control all anger, resentment, and wrath.

Prayer: Dear heavenly Father, help me to overcome all feelings of anger and wrath. Such feelings have truly tormented me, and I know they are not your will for me. I never want to grieve your Holy Spirit. Help me to put away all bitterness, wrath, anger, and all malice. With your help, Father, I will be kind to others, tenderhearted, and forgiving toward others, even as you have forgiven me.

Help me never to let the sun go down upon my anger. I know that you have not appointed me to wrath, but to obtain salvation through the Lord Jesus Christ. Thank you, Father. Realizing this, I now lift up my hands to you without wrath or doubting. Help me, Lord, to be swift to hear your Word, slow to speak, and slow to wrath, because I know that wrath never works your righteousness.

Keep me from all anger and pride, Father. I do not want to stir up strife or abound in transgression. I know that pride will bring me low. Your Word tells me that anger rests in the bosom of fools. Because I know this is true, and I do not want to be a fool, I choose not to be angry any longer.

Lord, I will trust in you and do good. I will delight myself in you and commit my ways unto you. I will rest in you and wait patiently for you. I will not fret over those who prosper even though they do not know you. I will endeavor to witness to them, and I will cease from anger and forsake all wrath.

Thank you, Father, for being merciful and gracious, slow to anger and plenteous in mercy. I want to be like you. Your Word declares to me that he who is slow to anger is better than the mighty. Help me to rule my spirit, Lord.

Scriptures: Ephesians 4:30-32; Ephesians 4:26; 1 Thessalonians 5:9; 1 Timothy 2:8; James 1:19; Proverbs 29:22-23; Ecclesiastes 7:9; Psalm 37:3-8; Psalm 103:8; Proverbs 16:32.

Personal Affirmation: I choose to lay aside the sin of anger, which besets me so easily, and I will run with patience the race that is set before me, looking unto Jesus, the Author and Finisher of my faith. (See Hebrews 12:1-2.)

Reflection: *"Anger is a short madness"* (Horace).

3

※

ANXIETY AND STRESS

Be careful for nothing; but in every thing by prayer and supplication with thanksgiving let your requests be made known unto God. And the peace of God, which passeth all understanding, shall keep your hearts and minds through Christ Jesus.

(Philippians 4:6-7)

Central Focus: Because I know anxiety and stress are harmful to me both physically and spiritually I will lean upon God to help me overcome them. Those negative forces will have no place in my life.

Prayer: Abba, Father, I love you and need you. Because I know you are near, I will be anxious for nothing, but in everything by prayer and supplication, with thanksgiving, I will let my requests be made known to you. As I do so, I know your supernatural and wonderful peace that surpasses all understanding will guard my heart and my mind through Christ Jesus.

53

Thank you for all the promises of your Word. I know they are yes and amen in Christ Jesus. Because I believe them, I will not worry about my life, because I know you will take care of me. I cast all my cares upon you, because I know you care for me. As I come unto you, Lord Jesus, I experience the rest you give to me. I take your yoke upon myself and I choose to learn of you, for your yoke is easy and your burden is light.

Throughout this day I will seek first your kingdom and your righteousness, because I know the result will be that you will supply all my needs. Thank you, Father.

I cast my burdens upon you, Lord, for I know you will sustain me, and I believe your promise that you will not permit me to be moved. I take my stand upon your Word, Father, and, as I do so, the stress I have been feeling is leaving me. Thank you, Lord, for freeing me from all anxiety and stress.

Father, I want your Word to bear fruit in my life. Therefore, I renounce the cares of this world, the deceitfulness of riches, and all kinds of lust and wrong desires. Thank you, Lord, for giving me a sound mind. You have not given me a spirit of fear, but you have given me a spirit of power and of love. Praise your mighty name!

Therefore, I will not be ashamed of your testimony, my Lord. I choose to be a partaker of the afflictions of the gospel according to your power, O God. Thank you for saving me and calling me with a holy calling, not according to my own works but according to your purpose and grace. I now know that I do not have to experience stress any longer. In Jesus' name, Amen.

Scriptures: Philippians 4:6-7; 2 Corinthians 1:20; Matthew 6:25; 1 Peter 5:7; Matthew 11:28-30; Matthew 6:33; Psalm 55:22; Mark 4:19; 2 Timothy 1:7; 2 Timothy 1:8-9.

Personal Affirmation: "Thou wilt keep him in perfect peace, whose mind is stayed on thee: because he trusteth in thee" (Isaiah 26:3). I will walk in God's perfect peace, because I trust Him with all my heart.

Reflection: *"In comparison with this big world, the human heart is only a small thing. Though the world is so large, it is utterly unable to satisfy this tiny heart. The ever-growing soul and its capacity can be satisfied only in the infinite God. As water is restless until it reaches its level, so the soul has no peace until it rests in God"* (Sadhu Sundar Singh).

4

BITTERNESS

*Looking diligently lest any man fail of the grace
of God;lest any root of bitterness springing up
trouble you, and thereby many be defiled.*

(Hebrews 12:15, KJV)

Central Focus: Bitterness is a poison that is
ruining my life. Through God's grace I will rise
above it and walk in sweetness and light from
this time forward. I will be victorious over this
enemy.

Prayer: Heavenly Father, I come to you now
because I struggle with bitterness in my life, and
I know this is not your will for me. I do not ever
want to grieve the Holy Spirit through bitterness,
so I ask you to help me overcome all bitterness,
wrath, malice, and evil speaking. I want to be
kind to others, tenderhearted, and forgiving
toward others. Therefore, I ask for your grace to
help me.

With your help, from this point on I will be
vigilant to make sure that I do not fail your grace
by letting any root of bitterness spring up to

trouble me and defile others. Thank you for your help with this, Father.

My heart knows its own bitterness, Lord. Please remove all bitterness from me. I renounce all bitterness, envying, and strife in my life. I will not lie against the truth, for I know that bitterness, envying, and strife lead to confusion and every evil work.

Father, instead of bitterness, I want your wisdom from above, which is pure, peaceable, gentle, and easy to be entreated. It is full of mercy and good fruits, without partiality, and without hypocrisy. That's what I want, Father. Your Word asks this important question: "Does a fountain send forth at the same place sweet water and bitter?" My answer to this is found in my desire to let only sweet water flow forth from my life.

I do not want to spend my years in bitterness of soul. I now know that you are delivering my soul from the pit of corruption and you have cast all my sins behind your back. Hallelujah!

Father, thank you for delivering my soul from bitterness. In Jesus' name I pray, Amen.

Scriptures: Ephesians 4:30-32; Hebrews 12:15; Proverbs 14:10; James 3:16; James 3:17; James 3:11; Isaiah 38:15; Isaiah 38:17.

Personal Affirmation: No more bitterness in my soul! I will walk in peace and joy from this time forward.

Reflection: *"Rest is not a hallowed feeling that comes over us in church; it is the repose of a heart set deep in God"* (Henry Drummond).

BOREDOM

And let us not be weary in well doing:

for in due season

we shall reap, if we faint not.

(Galatians 6:9)

Central Focus: Serving God is a joyous adventure. Because I know this is true, I will resist the temptation to ever be bored.

Prayer: Almighty God, as I struggle with boredom in my life, I know this is not your will for me. I ask, therefore, that you would help me to remember that you have called me to bear fruit for you. I put my hand to the plow, Father, and I will not look back. I will lay aside the weight of boredom in my life and run with the patience the race that you have set before me. I will keep looking to Jesus, who is the Author and Finisher of my faith. Thank you, Father.

When I think about it, I realize that I should not be bored at all. I will study your Word, Lord, in order to show myself approved unto you, a workman who does not need to be ashamed. I want to be able to divide your Word of truth faithfully and carefully. I want to learn how to abide in you, Lord, and to let your words abide in me, because then I know you will give to me what I ask of you.

Fill me afresh with your Holy Spirit, Father, that I would be able to bear the precious fruit of your Spirit in all the relationships and responsibilities of my life—love, joy, peace, longsuffering, gentleness, goodness, faith, meekness, temperance. Against these things there is no law. Thank you, Father.

Thank you, Lord God, for giving me the power of your Spirit to enable me to witness about Jesus effectively. This I will do every day of my life. This is the confidence I have in you, that if I ask anything according to your will, I know you will hear me. And because I know you hear me, I know that I will have the petitions I put before you.

Father, I have no reason to be bored, because you are leading me to study your Word, do your work, be fruitful, witness to others, and spend much time in prayer. These are the things I will do, and I will have fellowship with you and others. In Jesus' name I pray, Amen.

Scriptures: John 15:8; Luke 9:62; Hebrews 12:1-2; 2 Timothy 2:15; John 15:7; Galatians 5:22-23; Acts 1:8; 1 John 5:14-15; 1 John 1:3.

Personal Affirmation: Realizing all that God has called me to do, I now know that I have no reason to be bored ever again. Boredom, be gone in Jesus' name.

Reflection: *"Love wakes much and sleeps little and, in sleeping, does not sleep. It faints and is not weary; it is restricted in its liberty and is in great freedom. It sees reasons to fear and does not fear, but, like an ember or a spark of fire, flames always upward, by the fervor of its love, toward God, and through the special help of grace is delivered from all perils and dangers"* (Thomas á Kempis).

6

BROKENHEARTEDNESS

The Spirit of the Lord is upon me,
because he hath anointed me to preach the
gospel to the poor; he hath sent me to
heal the brokenhearted. . . .
(Luke 4:18)

Central Focus: God anointed Jesus to heal the brokenhearted. I, therefore, give my broken heart to Him, and I believe He will heal me of my brokenheartedness.

Prayer: Heavenly Father, as you know, my heart is broken. I ask you to bind up my broken heart. Give me beauty for ashes, the oil of joy for my mourning, and the garment of praise for the spirit of heaviness. I thank you for Jesus, who is anointed by your Spirit to heal my broken heart. I ask you to do so now. Thank you, Jesus, for healing me.

As I fall upon my knees and spread out my hands to you, Father, I ask you to take all sadness and heaviness from me. Though my heart is broken and I am filled with gloom, I ask you to hear me, O Lord, for I know your loving-kindness is good. Turn unto me according to the multitude of your tender mercies. Do not hide your face from me, for I am nearly in despair. Hear me speedily.

Make me understand the way of your precepts, Lord. Though my soul melts with brokenheartedness, I ask you to strengthen me according to your Word. Thank you for your unfailing love and mercy, which are from everlasting to everlasting. I receive your love as I pray.

You are restoring my soul, Father, and I ask you to restore unto me the joy of your salvation. I rejoice to know that you are taking me from strength to strength, and from sorrow to joy. Your joy, O God, truly is my strength. In Jesus' name I pray, Amen.

Scriptures: Isaiah 61:1; Isaiah 61:3; Luke 4:18; Ezra 9:5; Psalm 69:16-19; Psalm 119:27-28; Psalm 103:17; Psalm 23:3; Psalm 51:12; Psalm 84:7; Esther 9:21; Nehemiah 8:10.

Personal Affirmation: God is binding up my broken heart. He is restoring life to me. In Him I find my strength.

Reflection: *"Joy is like a well containing sweet water. It is not enough to know the water is there or even to drill the well. If the well is to be useful,* *the water must be brought to the surface. Those who know Christ have found the source of joy"* (Charles R. Hembree).

7

BURNOUT

But they that wait upon the LORD
shall renew their strength; they shall mount up
with wings as eagles; they shall run, and not
be weary; and they shall walk, and not faint.

(Isaiah 40:31)

Central Focus: As I wait in the presence of the Lord, I know He will reignite me and that I shall burn for His glory and His purpose. My sense of burnout has taught me much about life and what really counts in life.

Prayer: Father God, restore unto me the years that the cankerworm and palmerworm have eaten. Thank you for sending Jesus, who came to give me more-abundant life. I receive His abundance as I pray. Thank you, Father.

I know it is not your will for me to continue in this burned-out condition. Lord Jesus, you are my Good Shepherd, and you have given your life for me. Thank you for loving me so much that you gave your life for me. The Holy Spirit, who raised you, Lord Jesus, from the dead, now lives in me, and I know He will quicken my mortal body.

The power of your Spirit within me is helping me to regain my perspective. Thank you, Father. I now offer my body as a living sacrifice unto you, for I know this is acceptable unto you, and this is my reasonable service to you. Therefore, I will not be conformed to this world any longer, but I will be transformed by the renewing of my mind, that I may prove what is your good, acceptable, and perfect will in my life.

I want to be renewed in the spirit of my mind, Lord God, and to be filled afresh with the Holy Spirit, that I would be able to produce His fruit in my life. Help me not to be weary in well-doing, for I know I shall reap in due season if I do not faint.

Your Son, my Lord and Savior Jesus Christ, invites me, "Come unto me, all ye that labor and are heavy laden, and I will give you rest. Take my yoke upon you, and learn of me, for I am meek and lowly in heart, and ye shall find rest for your souls. For my yoke is easy, and my burden is light." As I do so now, Father, I am experiencing your wonderful rest. Thank you for lightening my burden. In the name of Jesus I pray, Amen.

Scriptures: Joel 1:4; John 10:10; John 10:11; Romans 8:11; Romans 12:1; Romans 12:2; Ephesians 4:23; Galatians 5:22-23; Galatians 6:9; Matthew 11:29.

Personal Affirmation: I am coming out of the burn-out phase of my life and accepting the challenges of God's Word to be fruitful and to be victorious. God is reigniting my spirit so that I can go forth for Him with the fire of His glory blazing all around me.

Reflection: *"God has not called me to be successful; He has called me to be faithful"* (Mother Teresa).

8

CONCEIT

Pride goeth before destruction, and

an haughty spirit before a fall.

(Proverbs 16:18)

Central Focus: I know I have no reason to be conceited. All I am and have belongs to God and comes from Him. I repent of my pride.

Prayers: Dear God, others have said I am conceited and stuck up, and I know this is sometimes true of me. Please forgive me of my sin and cleanse me from all unrighteousness. I know that pride is an evil work that comes from the devil, and because I fear you, Father, I now hate all forms of evil, including all pride and arrogance.

Thank you for showing me in your Word that shame always comes after pride. Your Word also declares that pride causes contention. I want to walk in integrity, Father, and to let my integrity, not my conceit, lead me. I never want to be ashamed of anything or to be contentious with others.

You have revealed to me, also, that pride goes before destruction and a haughty spirit will cause me to fall. Father, I want to have a humble spirit, to be clothed in humility, and not to think of myself too highly. Help me, Lord, to never again let anything be done through strife or vainglory. Through your grace I will learn to esteem others as being better than myself in lowliness of mind.

Lord God, I want the mind of Christ to be within me, for He made himself of no reputation and took upon himself the form of a servant. He humbled himself and became completely obedient unto you. I want to follow His example in all things, Lord.

I voluntarily humble myself under your mighty hand, Lord God, and I know you will exalt me in due time. Thank you for this promise from your Word. In Jesus' name I pray, Amen.

Scriptures: 1 John 1:9; Proverbs 8:13; Proverbs 11:2; Proverbs 13:10; Proverbs 11:3; Proverbs 16:18; Proverbs 16:19; 1 Peter 5:5; Philippians 2:3; Philippians 2:5-8; 1 Peter 5:6.

Personal Affirmation: I renounce all pride and conceit in my life. I choose to replace my arrogance with humility. I will walk in humility from this time forward. God is clothing me with humility.

Reflection: *"Nothing is won by force. I choose to be gentle. If I raise my voice, may it only be in praise. If I clench my fist, may it be only in prayer. If I make a demand, may it be only of myself"* (Max Lucado).

CONFUSION

For God is not the author of confusion,

but of peace, as in all churches of the saints.

(1 Corinthians 14:33)

Central Focus: There is comfort in knowing that the confusion I've been experiencing does not come from God. Indeed, God is helping me to overcome it.

Prayer: My God, I know you are not the author of confusion, but of peace. I ask you to fill me with your peace during this time of confusion. Direct me, Father, as I place my trust in you. In you, O Lord, do I trust; let me never experience confusion again. Deliver me in your righteousness and cause me to escape from this confusion. Incline your ear to me and save me.

You are my strong habitation, dear God, and I know I can go continually to you. You are my Rock and my fortress. Help me to walk in your wisdom, Father, because I know your wisdom is pure, peaceable, gentle, easy to be entreated, full of mercy and good fruits, and is without partiality and hypocrisy.

I believe in the Lord Jesus Christ, and I know this will keep me from all confusion. I need your wisdom, Father, and I ask you to impart your wisdom to me through faith. I know you will give it to me. I choose not to waver through confusion any longer, and I will no longer be double-minded, because I realize that a double-minded person is unstable in all his ways.

Renew my mind, dear Father, as I present my body and mind as living sacrifices unto you. I determine not to be conformed to this world any longer; through your grace I will be transformed by the renewing of my mind, that I may prove what is your good, acceptable, and perfect will in my life.

Dear Father, I thank you for delivering me from all confusion. You are the God of all grace, and you have called me unto your eternal glory by Christ Jesus. I ask you to perfect, establish, strengthen, and settle me. To you be glory and dominion forever and ever. In Jesus' name, Amen.

Scriptures: 1 Corinthians 14:33; Proverbs 3:5-6; Psalm 71:1; Psalm 71:2; Psalm 71:3; James 3:17; 1 Peter 2:6; James 1:5-8; Romans 12:1-2; 1 Peter 5:10-11.

Personal Affirmation: My God is not the author of confusion. I commit my way unto Him, and I know He will direct my paths without any confusion or uncertainty whatsoever. (See Psalm 37:5.)

Reflection: *"Faith's eye sees in the dark. It is a God-given eye, and it is like the eye of God"* (Charles H. Spurgeon).

10

DEFENSIVENESS

My defence is of God, which saveth
the upright in heart.

(Psalm 7:10)

Central Focus: I need to stop trying to defend myself, because God wants to defend me. I realize that His defense is far better than anything I have to offer. I turn away from my sensitivity and defensiveness through His mighty power.

Prayer: Dear Father in Heaven, I want to become less defensive in all my dealings with others. I want you to be my defense. I will wait upon you, Lord, and, as I do so, I receive your strength in my life. You are my defense and my strength, and I will sing unto you. You are my Rock and my salvation, and I know you are my defense, as well. Therefore, I shall not be moved.

Through you, dear Father, I shall do valiantly, for I know it is you who will tread down my enemies. Thank you, Lord.

I will let you arise in my life, dear Lord, and, as you do so, all my enemies shall be scattered. I want all my ways to please you, Lord. As a result, I know you will make even my enemies be at peace with me. Help me to remember that the battle is yours, not mine.

I want to be like Jesus, who tells me to not to strike back. If someone strikes me on the right cheek, I should turn the other one to him, as well. I realize that I need an attitude adjustment, Lord, that will enable me to love my enemies, bless them that curse me, and do good to those who despitefully use me and persecute me.

Keep me from all defensiveness, Father.

Scriptures: Psalm 7:10; Psalm 59:9; Psalm 59:17; Psalm 62:2; Psalm 60:12; Psalm 68:1; Proverbs 16:7; 1 Samuel 17:47; Matthew 5:39; Matthew 5:44-45.

Personal Affirmation: I surrender my right to self-defense to my heavenly Father, for I know He will always defend me and fight my battles for me.

Reflection: *"Goodness is something so simple; always to live for others, never to seek one's own advantage"* (Dag Hammarskjold).

11

DISCONTENTEDNESS

But godliness with contentment is great gain.

(1 Timothy 6:6)

Central Focus: Why should I feel discontented? God is my portion and the strength of my life. He is teaching me how to be contented in whatever state I find myself. (See Philippians 4:11.)

Prayer: Dear heavenly Father, I know that you do not want me to feel discontented. Help me always to remember that godliness with contentment is great gain for me. I want to be like the Apostle Paul, who said, "For I have learned, in whatsoever state I am, therewith to be content." I thank you for the sense of peace and contentment I am receiving as I pray.

Lord God, I know you will keep me in perfect peace as I keep my mind stayed on you, because I trust you. I want to trust you with all my heart, without leaning upon my own understanding. In all my ways, I will acknowledge you, and I know you will direct my steps.

Thank you for giving your peace to me. You don't give as the world gives, Lord, and because of your peace, I have no need to be troubled, discontented, or afraid. Thank you, Lord, for enabling me to be without anxiety about anything. In everything by prayer and supplication with thanksgiving I will let my requests be made known unto you. As a result, your wonderful peace, which surpasses all understanding, will guard my heart and my mind through Christ Jesus.

Thank you for sending Jesus, who came that I might have life, and that I might have a more abundant life! The abundance you give to me keeps me from being discontented. Thank you, Father.

Father, you supply all my needs according to your riches in glory by Christ Jesus. It is certain that I brought nothing into this world and I will carry nothing out. Having food and clothing, I will be a contented person.

Thank you for the peace and contentment you have brought to me. In Jesus' name, Amen.

Scriptures: 1 Timothy 6:6; Philippians 4:11; Isaiah 26:3; Proverbs 3:5-6; John 14:27; Philippians 4:6-7; John 10:10; Philippians 4:19; 1 Timothy 6:7; 1 Timothy 6:8.

Personal Affirmation: I am resolved to be content in whatever state I find myself. Discontentedness is now gone from my life forever. (See Philippians 4:11.)

Reflection: *"In Christ we are relaxed and at peace in the midst of the confusions, bewilderments, and perplexities of this life. The storm rages, but our hearts are at rest. We have found peace—at last!"* (Billy Graham).

12

DISCOURAGEMENT

Be strong and of good courage, fear not,
nor be afraid of them: for the LORD thy
God, he it is that doth go with thee; he
will not fail thee, nor forsake thee.

(Deuteronomy 31:6)

Central Focus: When I look at the situation thoroughly, I realize I have no cause for discouragement whatsoever. will encourage myself in the Lord, my God.

Prayer: Father God, as I read your Word, I realize I have no reason to feel discouraged. Help me to be strong and of good courage and not to fear, for I know you are with me, you will not fail me, and you will not forsake me. I choose to wait on you, Lord, and to be of good courage, for I know that you will strengthen my heart. Praise your mighty name!

Through your grace I will be strong and I will be encouraged, that I may observe to follow all your principles, which Moses brought forth. I will not turn aside from your commandments, Father, that I might prosper wherever I go.

Your Word is a great source of encouragement to me. I will meditate upon its precepts both night and day, and as I obey your commands, I know you will make my way prosperous and give me good success. Hallelujah!

One of your commands, Father, tells me not to fear nor be discouraged. With your help, I will obey this command at all times. As David did, I will encourage myself in you, O Lord. Indeed, I am encouraged by your law.

Abba Father, I will rejoice in you forevermore. Even though I have never seen the Lord Jesus Christ face to face, I love Him. Believing in Him, I rejoice with unspeakable joy that's full of glory. Forgetting those things that are behind, and reaching forth unto those things which are before, I press toward the mark for the prize of the high calling of God in Christ Jesus.

Thank you for replacing my discouragement with great encouragement through faith. In Jesus' name I pray, Amen.

Scriptures: Deuteronomy 31:6; Psalms 27:14; Joshua 1:7; Joshua 1:8; Deuteronomy 1:21; 1 Samuel 30:6; 2 Chronicles 31:4; 1 Thessalonians 5:16; 1 Peter 1:8; Philippians 3:13-14.

Personal Affirmation: I have no reason whatsoever to be discouraged, as I encourage myself in the Lord. The sense of discouragement I had been feeling is from the enemy, and I will resist him through the power of the Lord's blood.

Reflection: *"The ideals which have lighted my way, and time after time have given me new courage to face life cheerfully, have been kindness, beauty, and truth"* (Albert Einstein).

13

DISMAY

Fear not, nor be dismayed, be strong
and of good courage: for thus shall the
LORD do to all your enemies
against whom ye fight.

(Joshua 10:25)

Central Focus: My sense of dismay stems in part from fear, which I know is not God's will for me. His perfect love has cast all fear away from me. (See 1 John 4:18.)

Prayer: Abba Father, I know there should be no reason for dismay in my life whatsoever, for dismay involves fear, discouragement, and apprehension. I know you are with me, Lord, and you are going before me. You will never fail me nor forsake me. Because I know these truths, I will not fear or be dismayed about anything.

Through your grace I will be strong and of good courage. I will not be afraid or dismayed, for I know you go with me wherever I am. Give me wisdom and understanding, Father, and help me to obey your principles. I want to fulfill your statutes. As I do so, I know I will have your strength and courage, and I will have no reason to be filled with dread and dismay.

Help me to always remember that the battle is not mine, but it is yours. You are Almighty God, and I know you will strengthen me and help me. Thank you for upholding me with the right hand of your righteousness.

Help me to encourage myself, Lord, as the men of Israel did. Help me to be like David, who encouraged himself in you.

I realize that there is no reason for dismay when I consider the truth that I am more than a conqueror through Christ who loves me. I am fully persuaded, Father, that nothing shall be able to separate me from your love, which is in Christ Jesus, my Lord.

Because I am born of you, Father, I know I can overcome the world through faith. Because this is true, I know I have no reason to be dismayed or fearful any longer.

Scriptures: Deuteronomy 31:8; Joshua 1:9; 1 Chronicles 22:12-13; 2 Chronicles 20:15; Isaiah 41:10; Judges 20:22; 1 Samuel 30:6; Romans 8:37; Romans 8:39; 1 John 5:4-5.

Personal Affirmation: I will no longer be

dismayed about anything, for I know God is always with me. He is my light and my salvation. Of what then shall I be afraid? (See Psalm 27:1.)

Reflection: *"When you get into a tight place and everything goes against you, till it seems as though you could not hang on a minute longer, never give up then, for that is just the place and time that the tide will turn"* (Harriet Beecher Stowe).

DOUBT

Lord, I believe; help thou my unbelief.

(Mark 9:24)

Central Focus: The Word of God builds my faith. It is a bulwark against all doubt. I will immerse myself in God's Word through prayer and meditation.

Prayer: Dear Father in Heaven, I ask you to forgive me of all doubting and to cleanse me from all unrighteousness. Help me in this area of unbelief. I want to believe all the promises of your Word, which are Yes and Amen in Christ Jesus. I want to be like Abraham, who did not stagger at your promises, but was strong in faith, giving glory to you.

Help me to walk in faith, dear God. Help me to stand fast in the faith and to be strong. I thank you, Father, that I am crucified with Christ. Nevertheless I live. It is not I who lives, though; it is Christ who lives in me, and the life which I now live in the flesh I live by the faith of your Son, who loved me, and gave himself for me. Thank you, Father.

Therefore, I take up the shield of faith with which I will quench all the fiery darts of the wicked one, including doubt. Help me to continue in the faith, grounded and settled, and keep me from being moved away from the hope of the gospel.

Keep me from all double-mindedness, Father, for I know that a person who is double-minded is unstable in all his ways. Help me always to remember that faith is the victory that overcomes the world, and it is the substance of things hoped for and the evidence of things not seen. In Jesus' glorious name I pray, Amen.

Scriptures: 1 John 1:9; Mark 9:24; 2 Corinthians 1:20; Romans 4:20; 2 Corinthians 5:7; 1 Corinthians 16:13; Galatians 2:20; Ephesians 6:16; Colossians 1:23; James 1:8; 1 John 5:4; Hebrews 11:1.

Personal Affirmation: Doubt, be gone in Jesus' name! I choose to walk in faith from this time forward.

Reflection: *"The final test of religious faith...is whether it will enable men to endure insecurity without complacency or despair, whether it can so interpret the ancient verities that they will not become mere escape hatches from responsibilities but instruments of insights into what civilization means"* (Reinhold Niebuhr).

15

ENVY

For where envying and strife is, there is

confusion and every evil work.

(James 3:16)

Central Focus: Envy is a monster that is stealing life from me. In order to live the abundant life that Jesus wants me to have I must have all envy uprooted from my life. With His help it will be gone!

Prayer: Dear Father, my heart is sometimes filled with envy, I'm sorry to confess. Please forgive me and cleanse me from all unrighteousness. I believe your Word, which tells me that a sound heart is the life of the flesh, but envy is the rottenness of the bones. I want a sound heart, Lord.

Keep me from pride, arguments, and strife, Father, because I know that envy often stems from these sins. It is my choice to walk honestly, not in strife and envy. Help me, Father, and keep me from being carnally minded, for I know to be carnally minded is death. Instead, I want to be spiritually minded, for this brings forth life and peace.

Through your grace, I no longer have any desire for vainglory, Lord, and I do not want to provoke others or be envious of them. I want to be wise and to show forth your works in meekness instead of living in the bitterness of envy and strife.

Help me to walk in the Spirit, Father, so that I will not fulfill the lusts of my flesh. Thank you for the Spirit of life in Christ Jesus that has set me free from the law of sin and death. Help me to mortify envy and all the misdeeds of my body and soul, so I shall live. Thank you for leading me, for as many as are led by the Spirit of God are your children.

I love you, Father, and I thank you for delivering me from envy. In the mighty name of Jesus I pray, Amen.

Scriptures: 1 John 1:9; Proverbs 14:30; 1 Timothy 6:4; Romans 13:13; Romans 8:6; Galatians 5:26; James 3:14; Galatians 5:16; Romans 8:2; Romans 8:13-14.

Personal Affirmation: Envy's destructive power will no longer be a part of my life. I renounce it and walk away from it now.

Reflection: *"Envy and wrath shorten the life, and carefulness bringeth age before the time"* (Ecclesiasticus 30:24).

16

FATIGUE

But they that wait upon the Lord
shall renew their strength;
they shall mount up with wings as eagles;
they shall run, and not be weary;
and they shall walk, and not faint.

(Isaiah 40:31)

Central Focus: God is the strength of my life, and He is girding me with strength. He will surely overcome my fatigue and tiredness.

Prayer: Dear Father, I thank you for all the promises of your Word. As I wait upon you, help me to renew my strength, to mount up with wings as eagles, to run and not be weary, and to walk and not faint. I need your strength, Lord God.

I love you, O Lord, my strength. Thank you for girding me with strength. Help me never to be weary in well-doing. I seek you and your strength, O Lord. Thank you for your joy, which is my strength. I trust in you, because I know your strength is great.

Lord, you are the strength of my life. For this reason I will not be weary or afraid. Thank you for making your strength perfect in the midst of my weakness. Have mercy upon me, O Lord, for I am weak and weary. O Lord, heal me, I pray.

I thank you, Father, that your weakness is stronger than men. Thank you for being with me during this time of weakness, fear, and fatigue. Build my faith, Lord, so I will be made strong in spite of my weakness. Help me to wax valiant in fight and turn to flight the armies of the aliens. In Jesus' name I pray, Amen.

Scriptures: Isaiah 40:31; Psalm 18:2; Psalm 18:1; Psalm 18:39; 2 Thessalonians 3:13; 1 Chronicles 16:11; Nehemiah 8:10; Job 39:11; Psalm 27:1; 2 Corinthians 12:9; Psalm 6:2; 1 Corinthians 1:25; 1 Corinthians 2:3.

Personal Affirmation: I rise up out of my weakness and fatigue. I now lay aside every weight and the sin that easily besets me, and I run with patience the race that is set before me, looking unto Jesus, the author and finisher of my faith. (See Hebrews 12:1.) God's strength is pouring into me.

Reflection: *"'Be strong' and 'stand in the faith' are one and the same command"* (Paul Tillich).

17

FEAR

There is no fear in love; but perfect love
casteth out fear: because fear hath torment.
He that feareth is not made perfect in love.

(1 John 4:18)

Central Focus: I will learn to face my fears through the strength and love God has provided for me. All fear, be gone!

Prayer: Heavenly Father, I know that the fear I am experiencing is not from you. I know you love me, and there is no fear in your love. I praise you that your perfect love has cast out all fear from my life. I love you, because you first loved me. Lord, you are my light and my salvation, and because I know this is true, I will not fear others or anything. You are the strength of my life. Therefore, I have no reason to be afraid.

With your help, I will not let my heart be troubled. I believe in you with all my heart. Thank you for your peace, which keeps me from all fear. I know, dear Lord, that you have made it possible for me to not be anxious or fearful about anything, because your peace, which surpasses all understanding, is guarding my heart and my mind through Christ Jesus.

Thank you for your promise to give me your perfect peace as I learn to keep my mind stayed upon you. I choose to keep my mind stayed on you and to think about the things that are true, honest, just, pure, lovely, and of good report. I can do all things through Christ who strengthens me. Without Him, though, I can do nothing.

Make me perfect in your love, dear God, and perfect your love in me. I rejoice in the certainty that you have not given me a spirit of fear, but of power, of love, and of a sound mind. I am yours, and you are mine. I take my stand against all fear. In Jesus' name, Amen.

Scriptures: 1 John 4:18-19; Psalm 27:1; John 14:1; John 14:27; Philippians 4:6-7; Isaiah 26:3; Philippians 4:8; Philippians 4:13; John 15:5; 1 John 4:18; 1 John 4:12; 2 Timothy 1:7.

Personal Affirmation: God's perfect love has cast all fear from my life. (See 1 John 4:18.)

Reflection: *"When one confers with Jesus Christ the perplexity goes, because He has no perplexity, and our only concern is to abide in Him. Lay it all out before Him, and in the face of difficulty, bereavement and sorrow, hear Him say, 'Let not your heart be troubled'"* (Oswald Chambers).

18

GLUTTONY/ OVEREATING

And they that are Christ's have crucified
the flesh with the affections and lusts. If we live
in the Spirit, let us also walk in the Spirit.

(Galatians 5:24-25)

Central Focus: God will help me gain self-control over my eating habits. I will learn to practice moderation in all things.

Prayer: Father, I thank you for the truth that the Spirit of life in Christ Jesus has set me free from the law of sin and death. Help me to rise above all carnal-mindedness. I want to be spiritually minded, Lord, and I know this will be the key to peace in my life. Thank you, Father.

Fill me afresh with the Holy Spirit that I might enjoy and produce His fruit in all the relationships and responsibilities of my life. Help me to bear the fruit of moderation, temperance, and self-control in all that I do, especially in the area of eating.

Father, help me to crucify my flesh with all its affections and lusts and to live and walk in the Spirit. I thank you for showing me that no temptation has overtaken me but such as is common to all. You are faithful to me, O God, and I know you will not permit me to be tempted beyond what I am able to bear. Thank you, Lord, for making a way of escape for me.

Help me to endure the temptation to overeat, Lord, because I know you will be with me when I am tried in this area, and you have promised to give me the crown of life. I love you, Lord. Whether I eat or drink I want to do so to your glory, Father, and I want to glorify you in all that I do.

Help me to work and eat with quietness, and never to be weary in well-doing. I praise you for all your great and precious promises, for it is by them that I am able to partake of your divine nature, having escaped the corruption that is in the world through lust. Therefore, I will give all diligence to add virtue to my faith, knowledge to my virtue, temperance to my knowledge, patience to my temperance, godliness to my patience, brotherly kindness to my godliness, and love to my brotherly kindness.

Hallelujah for the freedom you have given to me. Your Son, Jesus Christ, has set me free from gluttony, overeating, and any form of lustful indulgence. I am free indeed! In Jesus' name, Amen.

Scriptures: Romans 8:2; Romans 8:6; Galatians 5:22-23; Galatians 5:24-25; 1 Corinthians 10:13; James 1:12; 1 Corinthians 10:28; 2 Thessalonians 3:10, 13; 2 Peter 1:4; 2 Peter 1:4-7; John 8:36.

Personal Affirmation: I will stand fast in the liberty wherewith Christ has made me free, and I will not be entangled with gluttony or overeating ever again. (See Galatians 5:1.)

Reflection: *"He who reigns within himself and rules his passions, desires, and fears is more than a king"* (John Milton).

19

GOSSIPING

Let your speech be always with grace,

seasoned with salt, that ye may know

how ye ought to answer every man.

(Colossians 4:6)

Central Focus: Speech is a wonderful gift from God. I want to use this gift in ways that will please Him, and I know that gossiping will never please Him.

Prayer: My Father in Heaven, help me to control my tongue. I never want to gossip again. Instead, I want my speech to always be with grace and seasoned with salt, that I might answer others in the proper way. I want my tongue to speak of your Word, Father, to praise your name, to encourage others, and to pray without ceasing.

Help me, Lord God, in all things, that I would show forth a pattern of good works, incorrupt doctrine, gravity, sincerity, and sound speech that cannot be condemned. It is my desire to use great plainness of speech when I am sharing with others because of the hope I have within me. Help me, Father.

Help me to remember that sin can be found in a multitude of words. Let the words of my mouth and the meditations of my heart be acceptable in your sight, O Lord, my strength and my Redeemer. Help me always to remember that a soft answer turns wrath away. I want my tongue to use knowledge in the right way, Father.

Your Word tells me that a wholesome tongue is a Tree of Life, and I want my tongue to be wholesome at all times, Lord. May my lips serve to disperse knowledge, and may I never gossip about others. Let my cry come before you, O Lord. Deliver me according to your Word. My lips shall utter praise. My tongue shall speak of your Word, Father, for all your commandments are righteousness. Thank you, Father.

Scriptures: James 3:8; Colossians 4:6; Romans 10:8; Psalm 149:6; Proverbs 25:11; Titus 2:7-8; 2 Corinthians 3:12; Proverbs 10:19; Psalm 19:14; Proverbs 15:1-2; Proverbs 15:4; Proverbs 15:7; Psalm 119:169-175.

Personal Affirmation: I repent of my tendency to gossip about others, and I determine in my heart to use my tongue to edify, not to tear down.

Reflection: *"The capacity for self-control, the ability to master one's sinful impulses and deal* *with them constructively, is itself a crucial moral power"* (Will Herberg).

20

❧

HELPLESSNESS

Our soul waiteth for the LORD:

he is our help and our shield.

(Psalm 33:20)

Central Focus: I am not helpless, for God is my help. I will lean on Him for the help I need.

Prayer: O Lord my God, you are my help and my shield, and because this is true the feeling of helplessness I've been experiencing is a deception. I am not helpless, for you are a very present help to me. Because I know this is true, I will not fear.

I will lift up my eyes unto the Lord, for all my help comes from Him. He will not permit my foot to be moved and He will never slumber. Father, I thank you that I now know that my help is in your name. Lord, I will not fear, because I know you are always with me. I will not be dismayed nor will I feel helpless because you are my God. Thank you for strengthening me, helping me, and upholding me with the right hand of your righteousness.

Help me always to remember, Father, your wonderful invitation to come boldly unto your throne of grace, that I may obtain mercy and find grace to help in my time of need. Kneeling at your throne is where I will find all the help I need and, therefore, I will not feel helpless ever again.

Lord God, I thank you for your promise to help me. This assures me that I will not be confounded, confused, or feel helpless again. Therefore, I have set my face like a flint, and I know I shall not be ashamed. Hear me, O Lord, and have mercy upon me. Be my Helper. I thank you that you have turned my mourning into dancing and you have girded me with gladness.

I will sing praise to you forever, Father, and I will not be silent. O Lord my God, I will give thanks unto you forever. Hallelujah!

Scriptures: Psalm 33:20; Psalm 46:1; Psalm 46:2; Psalm 121:1-2; Psalm 124:8; Hebrews 4:16; Isaiah 50:7; Psalm 30:4; Psalm 30:11-12.

Personal Affirmation: I no longer feel helpless, for I know that God is my Helper and He is always with me to help me and sustain me.

Reflection: *"Faith in God is simply trusting Him enough to step out on that trust"* (Catherine Marshall).

21

HOPELESSNESS

For in thee, O LORD, do I hope:

thou wilt hear, O Lord my God.

(Psalm 38:15)

Central Focus: There is an anchor for my soul, and it is the hope that God gives to me. He is taking the sense of hopelessness from me.

Prayer: Abba, Father, I ask you to remove this sense of hopelessness from me, as I place my hope in you. I realize that I should not be feeling cast down or disquieted. I will hope in you, Lord, and I will praise you for your help. Indeed, you are the health of my countenance.

Sometimes I feel that my strength and my hope have perished, because of my misery. As I reflect upon you, though, I am humbled in my spirit, Lord, and this gives me hope. I realize that it is by your mercies that I am not consumed and I know your compassions never fail. Praise your holy name! Indeed, your mercies and compassions are new every morning, and your faithfulness is so great. Lord, you are my portion, and I will hope in you.

Thank you for restoring hope to me, Father. My heart now rejoices and my tongue is glad. Now I know that my flesh shall rest in hope.

The hope you've given to me keeps me from being ashamed, because your love is shed abroad in my heart by the Holy Ghost, which you've given unto me. Thank you, Father. Your Holy Spirit within me causes me to rejoice in hope.

You are the God of hope, Lord, and you are filling me with all joy and peace in believing, that I may abound in hope through the power of the Holy Ghost. Thank you, Lord.

Now that you are restoring my hope, I ask that you would help me to use great plainness of speech as I deal with others so that they would experience hope, as well. Father, I ask you to make known the riches of the glory of your mystery to me, that I would know personally that Christ in me is the hope of glory. Help me to preach to others about Him, warning and teaching everyone in your wisdom, Father. I want to present everyone perfect in Christ Jesus.

Help me to maintain this diligence to the full assurance of hope unto the end. In Jesus' name I pray, Amen.

Scriptures: Psalm 38:15; Psalm 42:5; Psalm 42:11; Lamentations 3:18-26; Acts 2:26; Romans 5:5; Romans 12:12; Romans 15:13; 2 Corinthians 3:12, Colossians 1:27; Hebrews 6:11.

Personal Affirmation: God is filling me with hope. All hopelessness in gone, because I place all my hope in Him.

Reflection: *"Almighty God is on our team. He is our faithful Sustainer. When everybody else abandons us, we can count on Him. When nobody else is willing to endure with us, He is there. He is trustworthy, reliable, and consistent. We can depend upon Him"* (Charles Stanley).

22

INCONSISTENCY

Therefore, my beloved brethren,
be ye steadfast, unmoveable,
always abounding in the work
of the Lord, forasmuch as ye know that
your labour is not in vain in the Lord.

(1 Corinthians 15:58)

Central Focus: God is helping me to find greater steadness in my walk with Him. For too long I've been inconsistent in my Christian walk, and I know that this must stop. With His help I will prevail.

Prayer: Father God, help me to be steadfast, unmovable, and always abounding in your work. I never want to be inconsstent in my Christian walk again. With your help I will remain steadfast in my heart and I will have power over my will. Thank you for making me a partaker of Christ, as I endeavor to hold the beginning of my confidence steadfast until the end.

The hope you give to me, Father, is an anchor for my soul. It is both sure and steadfast. Thank you, Lord.

Give me your grace so I will be sober and vigilant, because my adversary, the devil, as a roaring lion, walks about, seeking whom he may devour. I will resist him by being steadfast in the faith. I will not be double minded any longer, Lord, because I know that a double-minded person is unstable in everything he does.

As I draw near to you, you are drawing near to me. Thank you for your cleansing power. Help me to purify my heart before you. Through your power I now lift up my hands, which were hanging down, and I receive your strengthening power. I will make straight paths for my feet.

Thank you for the great cloud of witnesses that encompasses me. Help me to lay aside every weight and the sin that does so easily beset me. Enable me, Father, to run with patience the race you have set before me and to look unto Jesus, the Author and Finisher of my faith, who for the joy that was set before Him endured the cross and is now sitting at your right hand.

Thank you for helping me to be your consistent witness, Lord God. In Jesus' name, Amen.

Scriptures: 1 Corinthians 15:58;   1 Corinthians 7:37;   Hebrews 3:14;   Hebrews 6:19;   1 Peter 5:9; James 1:4;   James 4:8;   Hebrews 12:13;   Hebrews 12:1-2.

Personal Affirmation: Through God's grace I know

I wil be consistent from this time forward. I will be steady in my walk with God.

Reflection: *"Beware of becoming careless over the small details of life and saying, 'Oh, that will have to do for now.' Whatever it may be, God will point it out with persistence until we become entirely His"* (Oswald Chambers).

23

INDECISIVENESS

Thy word is a lamp unto my feet, and

a light unto my path.

(Psalm 119:105)

Central Focus: Through God's grace I will not be indecisive any longer. I want all my choices and decisions to line up with God's Word. I have *decided* to follow Jesus in everything.

Prayer: Father, I thank you for your Word. It truly is a lamp unto my feet and a light unto my path. It presents your full counsel and will to me. I choose to walk in your Word, and this helps me to know that I will never be indecisive again. Thank you, Lord.

With your help, I will not be conformed to this world. Rather, I will be transformed by the renewing of my mind, that I may prove what is your good, acceptable, and perfect will. I thank you, God, for your promise that you will keep me in perfect peace as I keep my mind stayed upon you. This I will do, and I will trust you completely at all times.

Through your grace, Father, I will put off all indecisiveness and be renewed in the spirit of my mind. I want the mind of Christ to govern all my decision making from this time forward. Help me to gird up the loins of my mind, to be sober, and to hope to the end for the grace that is to be brought to us at the revelation of Jesus Christ.

Father, I will trust in you with all my heart and not lean upon my own understanding. In all my ways I will acknowledge you and I know you will direct my steps. Through faith and trust I will no longer be indecisive or double minded. I ask you for wisdom, Lord, your wisdom, and I know you will give it to me.

I ask you for your wisdom in faith, nothing wavering. I will seek you and your kingdom first, and I know you will add all other things unto me. Thank you, Father. Teach me your way, O Lord, and lead me in a plain path.

I choose to wait upon you, O Lord, and to be of good courage. As I do so, I know you will strengthen my heart and help me to be much more decisive. Praise you, Lord. In your name I pray, Amen.

Scriptures: Psalm 119:105; Romans 12:2; Isaiah 26:3; Ephesians 4:22; Philippians 2:5; 1 Peter 1:13; Proverbs 3:5-6; James 1:5; James 1:6; Matthew 6:33; Psalm 27:11; Psalm 27:14.

Personal Affirmation: No more indecision! From this point forward I will make my decisions in accordance with God's Word, and I know He will lead me every step of the way.

Reflection: *"Have patience with all things, but chiefly have patience with yourself. Do not lose courage in considering your imperfections, but instantly set about remedying them—every day begin the task anew"* (St. Francis de Sales).

24

INDIFFERENCE

That the members should have the same care

one for another. And whether one member

*suffer, all the members suffer with it; or one
member be honoured,*

all the members rejoice with it.

(1 Corinthians 12:25-26)

Central Focus: As a Christian, I must not be indifferent toward anything or anyone. With God's help I will put indifference behind me and maintain a good attitude.

Prayer: Father God, help me to overcome this sense of indifference toward others that I have been experiencing. Teach me how to suffer with the members of Christ's body who are suffering and to rejoice with those who are honored. As a member of the Body of Christ, I know I need to care more than I do.

Help me to be the kind of person who willingly bears the burdens of others and thereby fulfills the law of Christ. Help me to be sensitive toward others, and if I see someone who is overtaken in a fault or sin, to restore that person in a spirit of meekness, considering myself, lest I also be tempted in that area.

Fill me afresh with the Holy Spirit, Father, that I would produce His fruit in all the relationships of my life. I want to walk in love, joy, peace, patience, gentleness, goodness, faithfulness, meekness, and temperance. Help me to walk in the Spirit and to live in the Spirit.

Blessed be your name, Father. You are the Father of my Lord Jesus Christ, the Father of mercies, and the God of all comfort. You comfort me in all my tribulation, and this enables me to comfort others who are going through any difficulties with the same comfort you give to me. This is my desire, Lord, to be a caring person who gives comfort and encouragement to others.

Knit my heart together with other believers in the bond of love and unto all the riches of the full assurance of understanding, to the acknowledgement of your mystery, Father. Help me, Lord, to walk in mercy, kindness, humility of mind, meekness, and patience, forgiving others. Help me to put on the garment of love, Father, because I realize this is the bond of perfection.

I will let your peace rule in my heart and I will be thankful, as I let your Word dwell in me richly in all wisdom. From this time forward, Father, I want whatever I do in word or deed to be done in the name of the Lord Jesus, and I will always give thanks to you. In Jesus' name I pray, Amen.

Scriptures: 1 Corinthians 12:25-27; Galatians 6:2; Galatians 6:1; Galatians 5:22-23; 2 Corinthians 1:4; Colossians 2:2; Colossians 3:12-14; Colossians 3:15-17.

Personal Affirmation: I choose to put all indifference behind me and to walk in love toward others at all times. I will be a caring person from this time forward.

Reflection: *"The goodness of the Lord impels us to do good works. We have been conscripted to serve. Goodness does not make us 'goody-goodies,' but people who seek to know what is good for all and do it by Christ's power"* (Lloyd John Ogilvie).

25

IRRITABILITY

*Be careful for nothing; but in everything by
prayer and supplication with thanksgiving let
your requests be made known unto God.
And the peace of God, which
passeth all understanding, shall keep your
hearts and minds through Christ Jesus.*

(Philippians 4:6-7)

Central Focus: Irritability should have no place in my life. I renounce it now, as I seek God's help to overcome it.

Prayer: Father God, I repent of the irritability I have been experiencing and expressing, especially toward other people. I want to learn how to rejoice in you always. Help me not to be anxious or irritable about anything, but in everything by prayer and supplication with thanksgiving to let my requests be made known unto you. I know that as I do this, your peace, which surpasses all understanding, shall guard my heart and my mind through Christ Jesus. Thank you, Father.

I choose to cast all my cares upon you, for I know you care for me. O God of all grace, thank you for calling me unto your eternal glory by Christ Jesus. I know you will make me stronger despite the irritability I've experienced in the past, and you will establish, settle, and strengthen me. To you be glory and dominion forever and ever.

Father, with your help I will not let my heart be troubled by irritability any longer. I believe in you, and I believe in your Son, the Lord Jesus Christ. Thank you for your peace, which keeps my heart from being troubled.

Lord, through faith I will overcome all irritability in my life. Instead, I will do justly, love mercy, and walk humbly with you. Help me to regard all sources of irritation in my life as opportunities for growth, for I want to grow in grace and in the knowledge of my Lord and Savior Jesus Christ. To Him be glory both now and forever.

With your help I will let no corrupt communication proceed from my mouth, but only that which is good to the use of edifying, that it may minister grace to all who hear me. I will put away all bitterness, wrath, anger, malice, and evil speaking. Instead, I will be kind to others, tenderhearted, and forgiving toward others even as God for Christ's sake has forgiven me.

Scriptures: Philippians 4:4; Philippians 4:6-7; 1 Peter 5:7; 1 Peter 5:10; 1 Peter 5:11; John 14:1; John 14:27; Micah 6:8; 2 Peter 3:18; Ephesians 4:29-32.

Personal Affirmation: Irritability has no place in my life. Instead, I will let the peace of God rule in my heart. (See Colossians 3: 15.)

Reflection: *"Father, I thank Thee that there can be a total redemption from unpeace. Heal me at the depths, and then I shall be healed. Amen. Affirmation for the day: My depths are held by peace. The surface may be disturbed; it's the depths that count"* (E. Stanley Jones).

26

LAZINESS

And we desire that every one of you
do show the same diligence to the full
assurance of hope to the end: that ye be not
slothful, but followers of them who through
faith and patience inherit the promises.

(Hebrews 6:11-12)

Central Focus: Laziness is one of the Seven Deadly Sins. It has no place in my life. I will replace it with diligence, devotion, and steadfastness.

Prayer: Heavenly Father, I want to be your diligent servant, not a lazy person. With your help, I will be a follower of those who through faith and patience inherit your promises. Help me to keep my heart with all diligence, for the issues of life come forth from my heart. Help me to abound in faith, utterance, knowledge, diligence, love, and grace.

Father, your Word tells me that the way of a slothful person is a hedge of thorns, but the way of the righteous is a plain path. I want to walk in the path of righteousness for your name's sake. O Lord, I do not want to be lazy, because I know that a slothful person is the same as a great waster.

In your Word I find a great contrast between a righteous person and a lazy person. Whereas the lazy person covets greedily, the righteous person gives without sparing. I want to be a giver, Father, in the same way that you are. Indeed, I know you are the Giver of every good and perfect gift, the Father of lights with whom there is no variableness nor shadow of turning.

Help me to remember that you always bless the diligent, but that the lazy person will come to poverty. Through your grace, dear Lord, I will never be slothful again in any endeavor. Instead, I choose to be fervent in spirit as I serve you. I will rejoice in hope, be patient in tribulation, continue instant in prayer, and I will distribute to the necessity of the saints. Help me to always be hospitable, to bless them that persecute me, to rejoice with those who rejoice, and to weep with those who weep.

Scriptures: Hebrews 6:11-11; Proverbs 4:23; 2 Corinthians 8:7; Proverbs 15:19; Psalm 23:3; Proverbs 18:9; Proverbs 21:25-26; James 1:17; Proverbs 24:30; Romans 12:11-15.

Personal Affirmation: I renounce all tendencies to be lazy and I determine to be diligent from this time forward.

Reflection: *"Faithfulness is the quality of the friend, refusing no test and no trouble, loyal, persevering; not at the mercy of emotional ups and downs or getting tired when things are tiresome. In the interior life of prayer faithfulness points steadily to God and His purposes, away from self and its preoccupations"* (Evelyn Underhill).

27

LONELINESS

I will never leave thee, nor forsake thee.

(Hebrews 13:5)

Central Focus: Because I have a Friend that sticks closer than any brother and He is always with me, there is no reason to ever be lonely. I will reject that feeling when it tries to take hold of me.

Prayer: Heavenly Father, the loneliness I feel is dissipating as I draw near to you, because I know you are drawing near to me. I cleanse my hands and I purify my heart. As I do so, you are removing all double-mindedness from me. Thank you, Father.

Thank you for your promise that you will never leave me nor forsake me. I know you will be with me always, even until the end of the world. Because you are with me always, I know I have no reason for fear or any feelings of loneliness. I praise you for that certain knowledge, Lord God.

Even if I walk through the valley of the shadow of death, I will not be afraid of evil, for I know you are with me and your rod and staff bring me great comfort, O Lord. I ask that you would never be far from me.

In my time of loneliness, I will wait upon you, dear Lord, my Rock. Knowing that you are always there gives me great comfort. Thank you for being my faithful friend, one who sticks closer than any brother. Even when others forsake me, I know you will be right beside me.

From this point forward, I will do whatever you command me to do, because you have called me your friend. Thank you for letting me be your friend, Lord Jesus, and for letting me know what the Father has shared with you.

Thank you for choosing me and ordaining me to go and bring forth fruit. Thank you for promising that the fruit I bring forth will remain. Now I know that what I ask you, Father, in the name of Jesus, you will give to me.

I now ask you for friends. Help me to be friendly, so others will see you in me. I choose to be like Abraham, who simply believed you and it was imputed unto him as righteousness. Because of his faith, you called him your friend.

I now know I have no reason to feel lonely, for you are with me. Thank you, Father, for strengthening me with all might, according to your glorious power, unto all patience and longsuffering with joyfulness. I give thanks to you, Father, because I know you have made me a partaker of the inheritance of the saints in light, and you have delivered me from the powers of darkness and have translated me into the kingdom of your dear Son. This gives me the certainty that I will never be lonely again. In Jesus' name I pray, Amen.

Scriptures: James 4:8; Hebrews 13:5; Matthew 28:20; Psalm 23:4; Psalm 22:11; Proverbs 18:24; John 14:14-15; John 16:16; James 2:23; Colossians 1:11-13.

Personal Affirmation: I will never be lonely again, because I have a Friend who is closer than a brother. (See Proverbs 18:24.)

Reflection:

> "I know not where His islands lift
> Their fronded palms in air;
> I only know I cannot drift
> Beyond His love and care"
> (John G. Whittier).

28

LYING

*Let no corrupt communication proceed out
of your mouth, but that which is good to the
use of edifying, that it may minister
grace unto the hearers.*

(Ephesians 4:29)

Central Focus: My goal is to walk in truth and to never lie again, to use my tongue to glorify God and to build up others.

Prayer: Father God, I never want any form of corrupt communication to proceed from my mouth, including lying. Please forgive me for every lie I've ever told.

I want my communication to be yes, yes and no, no, for whatsoever is more than these comes from evil. I never want to bear false witness against another. May my tongue never speak or devise mischief in any form again. I do not want my words to ever work deceitfully. I choose to speak of your righteousness from now on.

Strengthen me according to your Word. Remove from me the way of lying. I have chosen the way of truth. I rejoice at your Word, Father. I hate and abhor lying, but I love your law. Deliver my soul, O Lord, from lying lips and from a deceitful tongue.

Lord, your Word clearly points out that you hate a lying tongue; it is an abomination unto you. I know this is true, so I will be careful from now on and will endeavor to speak only words of truth. Renew me in the spirit of my mind, Father, that I would put on the new man, which after you is created in righteousness and true holiness. Help me to put away all lying and to speak only truth.

Help me to know the truth, for it is the truth that will make me free. In the name of Jesus, who is the way, the truth, and the life, I pray. Amen.

Scriptures: Ephesians 4:29; Matthew 5:37; Exodus 20:16; Psalm 52:1-4; Psalm 119:28-30; Psalm 119:162-163; Psalm 120:2; Proverbs 6:17; Ephesians 4:22-25; John 8:32; John 14:6.

Personal Affirmation: From this time forward I will walk in truth, and I will never lie again.

Reflection: *"Kind words produce their own image in men's souls; and a beautiful image it is. They soothe and quiet and comfort the hearer. They shame him out of his sour, morose, unkind* *feelings. We have not yet begun to use kind words in such abundance as they ought to be used"* (Blaise Pascal).

29

MOODINESS

Thou hast put gladness in my heart,
more than in the time that their corn
and their wine increased. I will both lay me
down in peace, and sleep: for thou,
LORD, only makest me dwell in safety.

(Psalm 4:7-8)

Central Focus: The moodiness I've been exhibiting is not from God. I reject it and ask for His grace to overcome all moodiness in my life.

Prayer: Thank you, Lord, for putting gladness in my heart and taking away my moodiness and gloom. Hear, O Lord, and have mercy upon me; be my helper in overcoming the moodiness of my soul. Thank you for turning my mourning into dancing and girding me with gladness to the end that my glory may sing praise to you and not be silent. O Lord my God, I will give thanks unto you forever.

Thank you for anointing me with the oil of gladness, Father. Purge me with hyssop and I shall be clean. Wash me and I shall be whiter than snow. Make me hear joy and gladness, that the bones which you have broken may rejoice. Hide your face from my sins and blot out all my iniquities. Create in me a clean heart, O God, and renew a right spirit within me. Restore unto me the joy of your salvation and uphold me with your free Spirit.

Father, I know you are the God who made me. I am a sheep in your pasture. Therefore, I enter into your gates with thanksgiving and into your courts with praise. I am thankful to you and I bless your holy name. Lord, I love you, for I know you are good. Your mercy is everlasting and your truth endures to all generations.

Your joy is my strength, O Lord, and I want to walk in joy instead of the moodiness I've been experiencing. Lord, you are my Shepherd, and this causes me to know that I shall never want. You make me to lie down in green pastures, and you lead me beside the still waters. Thank you for restoring my soul, Lord, and for leading me in the paths of righteousness for your name's sake.

Surely goodness and mercy shall follow me all the days of my life, and I will dwell in your house forever. In Jesus' name I pray, Amen.

Scriptures: Psalm 4:7; Psalm 30:11-12; Psalm 45:7; Psalm 51:8-10; Psalm 51:12; Psalm 100:2-5; Nehemiah 8:10; Psalm 23:1-3; Psalm 23:6.

Personal Affirmation: I refuse to ever be moody again, because the Lord has given me gladness.

Reflection: *"The Christian owes it to the world to be joyful"* (A.W. Tozer).

30

MOURNING/GRIEF

Hear, O LORD, and have mercy upon me:
Lord, be thou my helper. Thou hast turned
for me my mourning into dancing: thou hast
put off my sackcloth, and girded me with
gladness. To the end that my glory may sing
praise to thee, and not be silent. O LORD my
God, I will give thanks to thee forever.

(Psalm 30:10-12)

Central Focus: Though grief and mourning are natural, they can be tempered by trusting in God with all our hearts. I choose to trust the Lord during this time of mourning and grief, realizing that the Lord will bring me through it.

Prayer: Father God, have mercy upon me and be my helper. Turn my mourning into dancing, I pray, and gird me with gladness, so that my glory may sing praise to you and not be silent. O Lord my God, I will give thanks to you forever. I look forward to the time when I will be able to return and come with singing unto Zion. At that time everlasting joy shall be upon my head, and

I will obtain gladness and joy, and all sorrow and mourning shall flee away.

You are unto me my everlasting light and my glory, Father. Thank you for your promise that the days of my mourning shall end. Thank you for pouring out your Spirit upon me and anointing me to preach good tidings to the meek, bind up the broken-hearted, proclaim liberty to the captives and the opening of prison to them that are bound, to proclaim the acceptable year of the Lord and the day of vengeance of our God, to comfort them that mourn.

Abba-Father, I ask you to give me beauty for my ashes, the oil of joy for my mourning, and the garment of praise for the spirit of heaviness, that I might be called a tree of righteousness, the planting of the Lord, so that He would be glorified in my life. Help me to be like a watered garden so that I would not sorrow any more. I ask that you would turn my mourning into joy. Comfort me, Father, and help me to rejoice in spite of my sorrow and loss.

Though I know that there is a time to weep and a time to laugh as well as a time to mourn and a time to dance, I ask, O God, that you would help me to rise up from my grief and mourning to praise you. Thank you for your wonderful promise of comfort, Father. This helps me to know that I am blessed even in my time of mourning.

In Jesus' name I pray, Amen.

Scriptures: Psalm 30:10-12; Isaiah 51:11; Isaiah 60:19-20; Isaiah 61:1-2; Isaiah 61:3; Jeremiah 31:13; Ecclesiastes 3:4; Matthew 5:4.

Personal Affirmation: In the midst of my grief and mourning I will praise the Lord. I receive God's comfort. In His presence there is fullness of joy and pleasures forevermore. (See Psalm 16:11.)

Reflection: *"But death is given no power over love. Love is stronger. It creates something new out of the destruction caused by death; it bears everything and overcomes everything"* (Paul Tillich).

31

NEGATIVITY

Finally, brethren, whatsoever things are true,
whatsoever things are honest,
whatsoever things are just, whatsoever
things are pure, whatsoever things are lovely,
whatsoever things are of good report;
if there be any praise, think on these things.

(Philippians 4:8)

Central Focus: As a Christian, I must remain positive. Negativity has no place in my life.

Prayer: Heavenly Father, help me get out of a negative mind set. I want to focus on the things that are true, honest, just, pure, lovely, and of good report. Lord God, you are the portion of my inheritance and of my cup. I know that you maintain my lot, and I have a goodly inheritance. Thank you, Lord. I will bless you for your counsel in my life.

I have set you always before me, and because you are at my right hand, I know I shall not be moved. Therefore, my heart is glad and my glory rejoices. My flesh rests in hope.

Thank you for showing me the path of life. In your presence there is fullness of joy, and at your right hand there are pleasures forevermore. Because this is true, I rise above all negativity and I have regained a positive perspective regarding everything in my life.

Lord God, you are my light and my salvation. Whom shall I fear? Lord, you are the strength of my life. Of whom shall I be afraid? I will extol you, O God, for you have lifted me up, and my foes will not rejoice over me. O Lord my God, I have cried to you and you have healed me. Hallelujah!

I will bless the Lord at all times. His praise shall continually be in my mouth. My soul shall make its boast in you, Lord. The humble shall hear thereof and be glad. I sought you, O Lord, and you heard me and delivered me from all my fears.

Have mercy upon me, O God, according to your loving-kindness. According unto the multitude of your tender mercies, blot out my transgressions. Wash me thoroughly from my iniquity and cleanse me from my sins, for I acknowledge my transgressions, and my sin is ever before me. Against you only have I sinned and been so negative in your sight. Forgive me, Father, and cleanse me from all unrighteousness.

I will sing of your mercies forever. With my mouth I will make known your faithfulness to all generations. Bless the Lord, O my soul, and all that is within me, bless your holy name. Bless the Lord, O my soul. I will not forget your benefits in my life. You have forgiven all my iniquities and you have healed all my diseases. You have redeemed my life from destruction, and you have crowned me with your loving-kindness and tender mercies. You satisfy my life with good things, so that my youth is renewed like the eagle's. God, I now know that I have no reason to be negative ever again. Thank you, Father.

Scriptures: Philippians 4:8; Psalm 16:5-9; Psalm 16:11; Psalm 27:1; Psalm 30:1-2; Psalm 34:1-4; Psalm 51:1-4; 1 John 1:9; Psalm 89:1; Psalm 103:1-5.

Personal Affirmation: From this time forward I will be positive in my outlook. I will no longer permit negativity to enter my soul.

Reflection: *"If you keep My commandments, you will abide in My love, just as I have kept My Father's commandments and abide in His love.*

These things I have spoken to you, that My joy may remain in you, and that your joy may be full" (John 15:10-11, NKJV).

32

NERVOUSNESS

Thou wilt keep him in perfect peace, whose mind is stayed on thee: because he trusteth in thee. Trust ye in the LORD forever; for the LORD JEHOVAH is everlasting strength.

(Isaiah 26:3-4)

Central Focus: The nervousness I've been experiencing is due to the fact that I have not remained close to the Lord. I will draw near to Him and, as I do so, I experience His peace and all nervousness evaporates.

Prayer: Lord God, thank you for your perfect peace which keeps me, as I keep my mind stayed on you. I trust you, Father, for I know you are my everlasting strength. Because I'm trusting you, I will not be anxious or nervous about anything. Instead, in everything by prayer and supplication with thanksgiving I will let my requests be made known unto you. As a result, I know that your perfect peace, which surpasses all understanding, will keep my heart and my mind through Christ Jesus.

Lord God, because I know you love me, I cast all my care upon you. Indeed, I cast my burden of nervousness upon you, and I know you will sustain me. I know you will never permit me to be moved. In you, Lord God, I will praise your Word. I put all my trust in you. I will no longer be fearful or anxious about anything.

I thank you that you have not given me a spirit of fear. Instead, you have given me a spirit of power, love, and a sound mind. Thank you, Father, for hearing me and delivering me from all my fears and worries.

With your help, dear Father, I will not let my heart be troubled, because I believe in you. Thank you for giving your peace to me. I know you do not give as the world gives, and because this is true, I will not let my heart be troubled or afraid any longer.

You, Lord, are my Shepherd. Therefore, I shall not want. You make me lie down in green pastures. You lead me beside the still waters. You restore my soul and lead me in the paths of righteousness for your name's sake. Yea, though I walk through the valley of the shadow of death, I will fear no evil, for I know you are with me. Your rod and your staff give comfort to me. Thank you for preparing a table before me in the presence of my enemies. You anoint my head with oil, and my cup overflows. Surely goodness and mercy will follow me all the days of my life, and I will dwell in your house forevermore.

Scriptures: Isaiah 26:3-4; Philippians 4:6-7; 1 Peter 5:7; Psalm 55:22; Psalm 56:4; 2 Timothy 1:7; Psalm 34:4; John 14:1; John 14:27; Psalm 23.

Personal Affirmation: Worry is counter-productive in my life. I replace all worry with God's wonderful peace.

Reflection: *When you come right down to it, nervousness is a sin because it stems from a lack of faith and trust.*

33

PASSIVITY

But thanks be to God, which giveth us the
victory through our Lord Jesus Christ.
Therefore, my beloved brethren, be ye
steadfast, unmoveable, always abounding
in the work of the Lord, forasmuch as ye know
that your labour is not in vain in the Lord.

(1 Corinthians 15:57-58)

Central Focus: How can I be passive when I realize my responsibilities as a believer? I must become an active Christian who is engaged in doing good and blessing others.

Prayer: Father, thank you for the victory you've given to me through my Lord Jesus Christ. Help me to be steadfast, unmovable, and always abounding in your work. I know that my labors are not in vain in you. Through your grace I will keep my heart with all diligence, for I realize that the issues of life stem from my heart.

I don't want to be a passive person, Father. Instead, I will be diligent, for I know that the hand of the diligent leads to prosperity, and it will rule. I thank you that the substance of a diligent person is precious.

It is a blessing for me to know that the thoughts of the diligent will lead to plenty. Help me to diligently seek good, Lord, for I know this will lead to your favor in my life. My heart's desire is to diligently obey your voice, O Lord.

Father, I know that it is impossible to please you without faith. I come to you with full belief in your existence, and I know that you are rewarder of all those who diligently seek you. I want to be a diligent seeker at all times, Lord.

Help me to be like Moses, Lord, for he endured, as seeing the One who is invisible—you! I see you by faith, Lord, and I want to endure to the very end. I now rise out of my passivity, laying aside every weight and the sin that does so easily beset me, and I run with patience the race you have set before me, looking unto Jesus who is the Author and Finisher of my faith.

Thank you for delivering me from all passivity, Father. In Jesus' name I pray, Amen.

Scriptures: 1 Corinthians 15:58; Proverbs 4:23; Proverbs 10:4; Proverbs 12:24; Proverbs 12:27; Proverbs 21:5; Proverbs 11:27; Zechariah 6:15;

Hebrews 11:6; Hebrews 11:27; Hebrews 12:1-2.

Personal Affirmation: Diligence shall be one of the central themes of my life from this time forward.

Reflection:

> *"Do all the good you can,*
> *By all the means you can,*
> *In all the ways you can,*
> *In all the places you can,*
> *At all the times you can,*
> *To all the people you can,*
> *As long as ever you can"*
> (John Wesley)

34

PERFECTIONISM

I am the vine, ye are the branches:
He that abideth in me, and I in him, the same
bringeth forth much fruit: for without me
ye can do nothing.

(John 15:5)

Central Focus: I am a human being, nothing more and nothing less, but the Perfect One lives within me and I will let Him live through me instead of trying to reach an unattainable goal of perfection.

Prayer: Lord, I want to abide in you, and I thank you for abiding in me. I want to be a fruitful believer, and I know that without you I can do nothing. Through you, though, I can do all things, because I know you strengthen me. Deliver me from perfectionism, Father, for I know this is a form of pride, and I also know that pride goes before a fall.

My reverential awe of you, Lord, causes me to hate all forms of evil, including perfectionism, pride, and arrogance. I realize that all these things are an abomination to you. Your Word teaches me that shame follows pride, and I do not want to be ashamed.

Perfectionism comes from deep within me. It was formed in my background. I know that it defiles me. Out of my heart evil thoughts, pride, foolishness, and so many other things flow. They come from my heart and they defile me.

Help me, Father God. Have mercy upon me. I confess my sin of perfectionism to you and I know you are forgiving me and cleansing me of all unrighteousness. Hear me when I call, O God of my righteousness.

All of my righteousness and perfectionism are as filthy rags in your sight. Have mercy upon me, O God, according to your loving-kindness. According unto the multitude of your tender mercies, blot out my transgressions. Wash me thoroughly from my iniquity and cleanse me from my sin, for I acknowledge my transgressions, and my sin is ever before me.

Father, thank you for delivering me from perfectionism. In Jesus' name I pray, Amen.

Scriptures: John 15:5; Philippians 4:13; Proverbs 16:18; Proverbs 8:13; Proverbs 11:2; Mark 7:20-23; Psalm 4:1; 1 John 1:9; Isaiah 64:6; Psalm 51:1-3.

Personal Affirmation: Thank God that I do not have to think I must be perfect any longer.

Reflection: *Perfectionism is a form of pride. "Self-knowledge puts us on our knees" (Mother Teresa).*

35

PESSIMISM

Rejoice evermore.

(1 Thessalonians 5:16)

Central Focus: The phrase "pessimistic Christian" is an oxymoron, for a Christian is intrinsically optimistic.

Prayer: Abba Father, I am happy to be your child. I realize that there is no need for me to ever be pessimistic, because I know you are for me, and if you are for me, who or what can be against me? Therefore, I will rejoice evermore.

Your kingdom in my life, Lord, does not consist of meat or drink, but of righteousness, peace, and joy in the Holy Ghost. Thank you, Father, for the joy you've given to me.

You are showing me the path of life, and I now understand that in your presence there is fullness of joy and at your right hand there are pleasures forevermore. I want to stay in your presence, Lord, and I know I will never be pessimistic again when I am in your presence.

I love you, Lord, even though I do not see you. I believe in you with all my heart, and I rejoice with unspeakable joy that is full of glory. Truly, my fellowship is with you, Father, and with your Son, Jesus Christ, and knowing this, my joy is full. Thank you for giving me your joy, Lord, which will remain within me and will always be full.

Lord God, your joy is my strength. Thank you for filling me with the Holy Spirit. His fruit in my life consists of love, joy, peace, patience, gentleness, goodness, faith, meekness, and temperance. Help me to produce the fruit of your Spirit in all the relationships and responsibilities of my life this day. Help me to share your fruit with others.

From this point forward, I want to walk worthy unto you with all pleasing, being fruitful in every good work, and increasing in my knowledge of you. Through your grace I will be strengthened with all might, according to your glorious power, unto all patience with joyfulness, and I will give thanks unto you, Father, because you have made it possible for me to be a partaker of the inheritance of the saints in light.

Scriptures: Romans 8:31; 1 Thessalonians 5:16; Romans 14:17; Psalm 16:11; 1 Peter 1:8; 1 John 1:3-4; John 15:11; Nehemiah 8:10; Galatians 5:22; Colossians 1:11-12.

Personal Affirmation: Jesus has transformed my life from being a pessimist to being a faith-filled optimist.

Reflection: *Faith leads to optimism, because faith knows the end of the story—a very positive conclusion indeed.*

36

REGRETFULNESS

Thou hast turned for me my mourning

into dancing: thou hast put off my sackcloth,

and girded me with gladness.

(Psalm 30:11)

Central Focus: Past regrets are but stepping stones to a happy and peaceful future. The regrets of the past have taught me so many things.

Prayer: Father God, help me to remember that I should not be focusing on the regrets of my past that stem from the mistakes I've made. Instead, I want to realize that you truly have turned my mourning into dancing, and you have girded me with gladness. Thank you, Father.

I confess my sins to you, including my mistakes and regrets—both my sins of omission and my sins of commission. Thank you for your promise to forgive me and to cleanse me from all unrighteousness. I receive your healing, cleansing, and forgiveness as I pray.

This one thing I do, forgetting those things which are behind, and reaching forth unto those things which are before, I press toward the mark for the prize of the high calling of God in Christ Jesus. From this point forward, I will no longer focus on my regrets nor be anxious about them. In everything by prayer and supplication with thanksgiving I will let my requests be made known unto you, Father, and I know your peace, which surpasses all understanding, will keep my heart and my mind through Christ Jesus.

Instead of concentrating on my regrets, I will think on things and ideas that are true, honest, just, pure, lovely, and of good report. Because of your mercies to me, Father, I now present my body a living sacrifice to you, holy and acceptable to you, for this is my reasonable service to you. I will not be conformed to this world; I will be transformed by the renewing of my mind, that I may prove what your good, acceptable, and perfect will for my life is.

I bless you, Lord God, with all that is within me. I will not forget all your benefits to me. You have forgiven all my iniquities and healed all my diseases. You have redeemed my life from destruction and crowned me with your loving-kindness and tender mercies. You have satisfied me with good things and you have renewed my youth like the eagle's.

Thank you, Lord. As far as the east is from the west, so far have you removed my transgressions from me. Thank you so much, dear Father.

I seek you and your strength, Lord. I will seek your face forevermore. I will remember your marvelous works and your wonders and judgments. Thank you for remembering your covenant with me.

You have taken my regrets from me, Father, and I will thank you forevermore. In Jesus' name I pray, Amen.

Scriptures: Psalm 30:8; 1 John 1:9; Philippians 3:13-14; Philippians 4:6-7; Philippians 4:8; Romans 12:1-2; Psalm 103:1-5; Psalm 103:12; Psalm 105:4-5.

Personal Affirmation: All my regrets have been covered by the blood of Jesus and they are buried in the depths of the deepest sea.

Reflection: *I am free from the guilt of the past and free from the fear of the future.*

37

REJECTION

To the praise of the glory of his grace,
wherein he hath made us accepted
in the beloved.

(Ephesians 1:6)

Central Focus: Because I know that God does not reject me, I am able to rise above the perceived rejection I have felt from others.

Prayer: Dear Father, I know that the feelings of rejection I've experienced are not from you, for I know you have accepted me in the beloved. Thank you, Father, for bringing me into your banqueting room where your banner over me is love.

I believe your promise, Father, that no weapon that is formed against me shall prosper, and every tongue that raises itself against me in judgment you will condemn. Thank you for the assurance that this is my heritage as your servant. Thank you for imparting your righteousness to me.

Thank you for making me perfect in love. There is no fear in your love, and I know that your perfect love casts out all fear from my life, including the fear of rejection. I love you, Lord, because you first loved me, and this knowledge helps me to understand that I need not fear rejection any longer.

I will praise you, for I am fearfully and wonderfully made. All your works are marvelous, Father, and my soul knows this truth very well. My substance was not hid from you when I was made in secret and curiously wrought in the lowest parts of the Earth. Your eyes did see my substance, yet being imperfect, and in your Book all my members were written.

I now know that I can be happy when I am rejected. Your Word tells me, "Blessed are ye, when men shall revile you, and persecute you, and shall say all manner of evil against you falsely, for my sake." I rejoice, Lord, and I am exceedingly glad, for I now know that my reward in Heaven is so great.

Thank you, Lord, for making me the salt of the Earth and the light of the world. From this time forward I will let my light shine before others, that they may see my good works and glorify you. In Jesus' name I pray, Amen.

Scriptures: Ephesians 1:6; Song of Solomon 2:4; Isaiah 54:17; 1 John 4:18-19; Psalm 139:14-16; Matthew 5:11-12; Matthew 5:13-16.

Personal Affirmation: Rejection no longer has a grip on my life. I have been set free from all rejection through the blood of Jesus and the grace of God.

Reflection: *"God is clearly deserving of our love especially if we consider who He is that loves us, who we are that He loves, and how much He loves us"* (St. Bernard of Clairvaux).

38

SADNESS/DEPRESSION

Be glad in the LORD, and rejoice, ye righteous:
And shout for joy, all ye that are
upright in heart.

(Psalm 32:11)

Central Focus: To know that God loves me with an everlasting love removes all gloom, sadness, and depression from my life.

Prayer: Almighty God, you are my reason for happiness. I realize that I have no reason to be sad when I am with you. Praise your holy name! Therefore, I choose to make a joyful noise unto you. My soul shall be joyful in you. I am filled with the comfort you have given to me, and I choose to be exceedingly joyful even in times of tribulation.

Help me to walk in your wisdom, Lord God, because I know this will restore happiness to me. Restore unto me the joy of my salvation and uphold me with your free Spirit. I now know that happiness comes from trusting in you, Father. Therefore, I choose to trust in you with all my heart, without leaning on my own understanding. In all my ways I will acknowledge you, and I know you will direct my steps.

Thank you for replacing my sadness with your joy, which is giving me strength. I will keep your law, and I know this will bring great happiness and joy to me. Thank you, Father. My happiness comes from knowing that you, the God of Jacob, are my help, and all my hope is in you. You made Heaven, the Earth, the sea, and all that there is.

Thank you, Father, that you will reign forever, unto all generations. I praise you, my Lord and my King.

Scriptures: Psalm 100:1; Isaiah 61:10; 2 Corinthians 7:4; Proverbs 3:13; Psalm 51:12; Proverbs 16:20; Proverbs 3:5-6; Nehemiah 8:10; Proverbs 29:18; Psalm 146:5-6; Psalm 146:10.

Personal Affirmation: "The joy of the Lord is my strength" (Nehemiah 8:10).

Reflection: *"I never take My joy away from you. It is always within you and can always be expressed in your life"* (Colin Urquhart).

39

SELF-CENTEREDNESS

I am crucified with Christ: nevertheless I live;

yet not I, but Christ liveth in me: and the life

which I now live in the flesh I live by the

faith of the Son of God, who loved me,

and gave himself for me.

(Galatians 2:20)

Central Focus: With God's help I will be Christ-centered instead of being self-centered.

Prayer: Heavenly Father, help me to realize more fully than ever that I am crucified with Christ and He lives within me. I praise you that the life I now live in the flesh I live by the faith of the Son of God, who loved me and gave himself for me. I know that without Him I can do nothing.

Instead of focusing on myself, I wil seek first your kingdom, Father, along with your righteousness. As I do so, I know you will take care of everything else. I know that anything in my life that is self-centered is prideful and unrighteous.

Thank you for revealing this truth to me: "Except a corn of wheat fall into the ground and die, it abideth alone: but if it die, it bringeth forth much fruit." Jesus said that if I love my life, I will lose it, but if I hate my life, I will keep it unto eternal life. I want to be a fruit-bearing Christian, Lord, and I want to keep my life unto eternal life.

Lord God, you are the vinedresser. Purge me of my sin, so I will bring forth fruit. Thank you for cleansing me through your Word. I will abide in you and let your Word abide in me. Without you I can do nothing.

I want you to be the center of my life, Lord God. In you, O Lord, I do put my trust. Let me never be ashamed. Deliver me in your righteousness. Bow down your ear to me. Deliver me speedily and be my strong rock. You are my fortress. For thy name's sake lead me and guide me.

I fear you, Lord, and I hate evil, especially my own self-centeredness, pride, lust, and arrogance. Thank you for the counsel and sound wisdom you have given to me through your Word. You are understanding and you have strength.

Forgive me of my self-centeredness, Father. I want you to be the center of my life. As I confess my sin to you, I know you are forgiving me and cleansing me from all unrighteousness. Praise your holy name!

Scriptures: Galatians 2:20; John 15:5; Matthew 6:33; John 12:24; John 12:25; John 15:1-5; Psalm 31:1-3; Proverbs 8:13; Proverbs 8:14; 1 John 1:9.

Personal Affirmation: I have decided to take the focus off myself and to turn my eyes upon Jesus.

Reflection: *"That man who lives for self alone lives for the meanest mortal known" (Joaquin Miller).*

40

SELF-CONSCIOUSNESS

That which cometh out of the man, that defileth

the man. For from within, out of the heart of men,

proceed evil thoughts…pride, foolishness: all these things

come from within, and defile the man.

(Mark 7:20-23)

Central Focus: Self-consciousness comes from the self-life, and it is a form of pride. I repent of all self-consciousness.

Prayer: Heavenly Father, my pride and foolishness that stem from self-consciousness defile me. I confess the sin of self-consciousness to you now, and I know you have forgiven me and cleansed me from all unrighteousness.

Lord, I realize that my self-consciousness is a work of my flesh, and I do not want to walk after my flesh any longer. Instead, I will walk after your Spirit. I know that those who walk after the flesh do mind the things of the flesh, but they that are after the Spirit, will mind the things of the Spirit.

Thank you for showing me the truth that to be carnally minded is death, but to be spiritually minded is life and peace. Father, I want the life and peace that come from being spiritually minded.

Self-consciousness comes from the carnal mind, and the carnal mind is enmity against you, Lord, because it is not subject to your law and cannot be. I know that I cannot please you, Father, if I am in the flesh.

Fill me with faith, Father, I pray. Thank you for showing me that it is impossible to please you without faith. When I come to you, I do so with full belief that you exist and that you are a rewarder of all who diligently seek you. Father, I will seek you with all diligence.

It is clear to me, Lord, that my self-consciousness has stemmed from a fear of others. With your help, I will no longer fear people—those who are able to kill the body, but not the soul. I will follow you, Lord, and I will deny myself, take up my cross, and walk with you. Thank you for pointing this out to me: "For whosoever will save his life shall lose it, but whosoever shall lose his life for your sake and the sake of the gospel shall save it." In Jesus' name I pray, Amen.

Scriptures: Mark 7:20-23; 1 John 1:9; Romans 8:4; Romans 8:5; Romans 8:6; Romans 8:7; Hebrews 11:6; Matthew 10:28; Mark 8:34-38.

Personal Affirmation: No longer will I let self-consciousness control me and negatively impact my relationships with others. I will be Christ-conscious instead of self-conscious.

Reflection: *Love is never self-conscious; it always reaches out to others.*

41

SELF-DESTRUCTIVENESS

Know ye not that ye are the temple of God,
and that the Spirit of God dwelleth in you?
If any man defile the temple of God, him shall
God destroy; for the temple of God is holy,
which temple ye are.

(1 Corinthians 3:16-17)

Central Focus: God wants me to treat myself with love. I hereby reject and renounce all tendencies to be self-destructive.

Prayer: Heavenly Father, I ask you to remove all tendencies toward self-destructiveness that I have been dealing with. Thank you for showing me that my body is your temple. This makes me realize that I must not defile or harm myself in anyway.

Thank you for buying me with the price of Jesus' blood. My goal from now on will be to glorify you in my body and in my spirit, inasmuch as both of them are yours. Because of your mercies to me,

Father, I present my body as a living sacrifice to you—holy and acceptable—for I realize that this is my reasonable service to you. From this point forward I will not be conformed to this world. Instead, I will be transformed by the renewing of my mind, that I may prove what is your good, perfect, and acceptable will.

Help me to remember, Lord, that the thief comes to steal, kill, and destroy, but you have come to impart abundant life to me. You are my Good Shepherd. Thank you for giving your life for me.

Realizing that those who are in the flesh cannot ever please you, Lord, I want to walk in the Spirit. Thank you for sending your Spirit to dwell within me. I am fully persuaded that nothing shall be able to separate me from your love, which is in Christ Jesus my Lord.

According to my earnest expectation and my hope, in nothing shall I be ashamed, but with all boldness, as always, Christ shall be magnified in my body.

Fill me afresh with your Holy Spirit, Father, that I may produce the fruit of the Spirit in all the relationships and responsibilities of my life—love, joy, peace, patience, meekness, gentleness, goodness, and self-control. I want to live in the Spirit and walk in the Spirit at all times.

Scriptures: 1 Corinthians 3:16-17; 1 Corinthians 6:19-20; Romans 12:1-2; John 10:10; John 10:11; Romans 8:7-9; Romans 8:38-39; Philippians 1:20; Galatians 5:22-23; Galatians 5:26.

Personal Affirmation: God has delivered me from all self-destructiveness. Praise His holy name. I will take good care of my body, that I might serve Him more fully.

Reflection: *Self-destructiveness always comes from the devil. I come against him in the name of Jesus.*

42

SELF-RIGHTEOUSNESS

But we are all as an unclean thing,
and all our righteousnesses are as filthy rags;
and we all do fade as a leaf; and our iniquities,
like the wind, have taken us away.

(Isaiah 64:6)

Central Focus: To be self-righteous is to be severely misled. The only righteousness I have has been imputed to me through the death of Jesus Christ.

Prayer: Father God, thank you for reminding me that all my righteousness is like filthy rags in your sight. Keep me from all self-righteousness, and help me to live by faith. I yield myself to you, Father, and I yield my entire being to you, that my life would be an instrument of righteousness to you.

Let your righteousness be fulfilled in my life, Lord, as I learn to walk not after the flesh, but after the Spirit. Thank you for sending Jesus, who has been made unto me righteousness, sanctification, and holiness. I will glory in Him, and never glory in myself.

I am now an ambassador for Christ, who was made sin for me, that I might be made your righteousness in Him. I put on the breastplate of righteousness that you have provided for me. Fill me with the fruits of righteousness, Father, which are by Jesus Christ, unto your glory and praise.

I want to be found in Christ, not having my own righteousness, which is of the Law. I want to walk in the righteousness that comes through the faith of Christ—the righteousness which is of God by faith. I will flee from all forms of self-righteousness and follow after your righteousness, godliness, faith, love, patience, and meekness.

Help me, Lord, to live unto righteousness, for it was through your stripes that I have been healed.

In Jesus' name I pray, Amen.

Scriptures: Isaiah 64:6; Romans 1:17; Romans 6:13; Romans 8:4; 1 Corinthians 1:30-31; 2 Corinthians 5:20-21; Ephesians 6:14; Philippians 1:11; Philippians 3:9; 1 Timothy 6:11; 1 Peter 2:24.

Personal Affirmation: I will walk in the righteousness of God from this time forward, because I have been delivered from self-righteousness. Praise the Lord!

Reflection: *"But enough! This is good and that is good; take away 'this' and 'that,' and gaze if you can upon good itself. Then you will behold God, good not through the having of any other good thing, but He is the goodness of every good"* (St. Augustine).

43

SENSITIVITY

My grace is sufficient for thee: for my strength
Is made perfect in weakness.

(2 Corinthians 12:9)

Central Focus: To be overly sensitive is to be weak and ineffective. Through God's grace I will overcome this tendency in my life and become strong in the Lord.

Prayer: Father, I ask you to deliver me from being so sensitive toward others. Give me your strength to overcome my sensitive nature. Help me to remember that though I walk in the flesh, I do not have to war according to the flesh.

Thank you for showing me that the weapons of spiritual warfare are not carnal, but they are mighty through you to the pulling down of strongholds, including the stronghold of sensitivity. Casting down imaginations and everything that exalts itself against knowing you, I now bring all my thoughts into captivity to the obedience of Christ.

Lord, I know that you are my light and my salvation, and because this is true I never need to fear others or to be overly sensitive. You are the strength of my life; of whom shall I be afraid? I will wait on you, Lord, and be of good courage. As I do so, I know you will strengthen my heart. Praise your holy name!

Cause me to hear your loving-kindness in the morning, for in you do I place my trust. Cause me to know the way in which I should walk, for I lift up my soul to you. Teach me to do your will, Lord God. Your Spirit is so good. Lead me into the land of uprightness.

Quicken me, O Lord, for your name's sake. For your righteousness' sake, bring my soul out of all its sensitivity, completely out of trouble. Help me to love all those whom I perceive to be my enemies, to bless them that curse me, to do good to those who hate me, and to pray for those who despitefully use me and persecute me, that I might truly live as your child, Father.

In Jesus' name I pray, Amen.

Scriptures: 2 Corinthians 12:9; 2 Corinthians 10:3; 2 Corinthians 10:4; 2 Corinthians 10:5; Psalm 27:1; Psalm 27:14; Psalm 143: 8; Psalm 143:10; Psalm 143:11; Matthew 5:44-45.

Personal Affirmation: The Lord has delivered me from all sensitivity toward others and their responses to me. I will walk in confidence from this time forward.

Reflection: *"Pour through me now; I yield myself to Thee, O Love that led my Lord to Calvary"* (Amy Carmichael).

44

SEXISM

There is neither Jew nor Greek, there is neither bond nor free, there is neither male nor female: for ye are all one in Christ Jesus.

(Galatians 3:28)

Central Focus: I want to love God with all my heart, soul, and strength, and to love all others as myself. I repent of the sin of sexism.

Prayer: Heavenly Father, thank you for showing me that both males and females are one In Christ Jesus. Deliver me from all sexism.

Let me walk in love without any hypocrisy whatsoever. I will abhor that which is evil, including sexism, and I will cleave to that which is good. Help me to be kind in my affections toward all others with brotherly love. In honor I will prefer others.

Fill me afresh with your Spirit, Father, that I would produce the fruit of your Spirit in all the relationships and responsibilities of my life—

love, joy, peace, patience, meekness, gentleness, goodness, faithfulness, and self-control.

Teach me how to love all others, Father, for such love is of you, and everyone that loves is born of you and knows you, for you are love. I thank you for showing me that there is no fear in love. Thank you for your perfect love, which casts out all fear.

It is my desire, Father, to fulfill your joy in my life. I never want to do anything through strife or vainglory, but in lowliness of mind I will esteem others (of both sexes) as being better than myself.

Help me to bear the burdens of others, and so fulfill the law of Christ. Help me not to grow weary in well-doing toward others, for I know I will reap in due season. Let me take every opportunity to do good to others, especially toward those who are of the household of faith.

Thank you for delivering me from sexism, Father. In Jesus' name I pray, Amen.

Scriptures: Galatians 3:28; Romans 12:9; Romans 12:10; Galatians 5:22-23; 1 John 4:7-8; 1 John 4:18; Philippians 2:2; Philippians 2:3; Galatians 6:2; Galatians 6:9-10.

Personal Affirmation: With God's help, I will treat all people equally and with the respect they deserve.

Reflection: *"But the fruit of the Spirit is love, joy, peace, longsuffering, gentleness, goodness, faith, meekness, temperance: against such there is no law"* (Galatians 5:22-23)

45

SHAME

There is therefore now no condemnation to them which are in Christ Jesus, who walk notafter the flesh, but after the Spirit.

(Romans 8:1)

Central Focus: My sense of shame has led me to Jesus Christ. In Him there is no shame.

Prayer: Heavenly Father, I thank you for the truth of your Word. Thank you for freeing me from all shame and condemnation, as I learn to walk in the Spirit. I praise you for the wonderful knowledge that the law of the Spirit of life in Christ Jesus has set me free from the law of sin and death (and all shame).

Lord, I have chosen the way of truth. I have laid your judgments before me. Do not let me be put to shame. I will run the way of your commandments, and you will enlarge my heart. Teach me, O Lord, the way of your statutes, and I shall keep them unto the end.

Keep me from all pride, Father, because I know that pride always results in shame. Let my integrity guide me in all things. Thank you for the promises of your Word, which teach me not to fear. You have assured me, Lord, that I shall not be ashamed. Thank you so much.

I rise up out of all shame, and I shall not be confounded any longer. You are my Redeemer, the Holy One of Israel, and the God of the whole Earth. I praise you, Father.

I thank you for the great cloud of witnesses that surrounds me. With your help, Lord, I will lay aside every weight and the sin that does so easily beset me, and I will run with perseverance the race you have set before me, looking unto Jesus who is the Pioneer and Perfecter of my faith. I want to be like Him, for He endured the cross, despised the shame, and is now set down at the right hand of the throne of God.

I will not ever be ashamed of the Gospel of Jesus Christ, which is your power unto salvation to all who will believe. Thank you for delivering me from all shame.

Scriptures: Romans 8:1-2; Psalm 119:30-33; Proverbs 11:2-3; Isaiah 54:4-5; Hebrews 12:2-3; Romans 1:16.

Personal Affirmation: The sense of shame and degradation that I had long experienced is gone forever! Hallelujah!

Reflection: *"Therefore if any man be in Christ, he is a new creature: old things are passed away; behold, all things are become new"* (2 Corinthians 5:17).

46

SHORT-SIGHTEDNESS

Where there is no vision, the people perish:

but he that keepeth the law, happy is he.

(Proverbs 29:18)

Central Focus: Short-sightedness stems from a lack of faith and purpose. I will capture the vision of the Lord and run with it.

Prayer: Father God, give me your vision and help me to walk in your law. Keep me from all short-sightedness and help me to be a forward-looking person. Forgetting those things which are behind, and reaching forth unto those things which are before, I press toward the mark for the prize of the high calling of God in Christ Jesus.

Thank you for showing me that I can do all things through Christ who strengthens me. Because I know this is true, I will set my affections on things above, not on things on the Earth.

Help me to walk worthy of you unto all good pleasing, being fruitful in every good work and increasing in your knowledge. Strengthen me with all might, Lord God, according to your glorious power, unto all patience and longsuffering with joyfulness.

I give thanks to you, Lord, for all you are doing in my life, for the vision you are giving to me, and for making me meet to be a partaker of the inheritance of your saints in light. Thank you for delivering me from the power of darkness, including all short-sightedness, and translating me into the Kingdom of your dear Son.

Help me to always remember that you are before all things and that by you all things consist. Help me to continue in the faith, grounded and settled, and prevent me from being moved away from the hope of the gospel.

I will stand my watch and take my place upon the tower. I will watch to see what you say to me, Father, and what I shall answer when I am reproved. I will write the vision you give to me and make it plain. I will run with your vision.

In the name of Jesus I pray, Amen.

Scriptures: Proverbs 29:18; Philippians 4:13; Colossians 3:2; Colossians 1:10-13; Colossians 1:17; Colossians 1:23; Habakkuk 2:1-3.

Personal Affirmation: I look forward to the future God has in store for me, and I will avoid all short-sightedness.

Reflection: *"For now we see through a glass, darkly; but then face to face: now I know in part; but then shall I know even as also I am known"* (1 Corinthians 13:12).

47

SINFULNESS

If we confess our sins, he is faithful and just to

Forgive us our sins, and to cleanse us from all unrighteousness.

(1 John 1:9)

Central Focus: Sin in my life has separated me from God and His wonderful peace. I lay aside all sin now, and I receive His peace. I repent of all my sins.

Prayer: My Father and my Lord, I come to you now with a heart that is full of repentance. I confess my sins to you, and I receive your forgiveness and cleansing from all my unrighteousness. Thank you for your healing power.

Though all have sinned, including myself, and have come short of your glory, and I know that the wages of sin is death, I thank you that you have given me eternal life through your Son, Jesus Christ, my Lord, who loved me and gave himself for me. I am crucified with Christ. Nevertheless I live, but it is really Christ who lives within me, and the life I now live is lived by the faith of the Son of God. Thank you, Father.

I praise you that you have shown me that I can cleanse my way by taking heed to your Word. I have hid your Word in my heart, that I might not sin against you. Help me to walk in the light, Father, as you are in the light. In this way I will have fellowship with others and with you. Thank you for the blood of Jesus Christ, which cleanses me from all sin.

I am fully persuaded, Father, that neither death nor life, nor angels, nor principalities, nor powers, nor things present, nor things to come, nor height, nor depth, nor any other creature, shall be able to separate me from the love of God, which is in Christ Jesus our Lord. Thank you for this fact of my faith, Father.

Help me to remember, Father, that you have forgiven me of my sins. They are buried in the depths of the deepest sea and you have removed my sins far from me. I realize that if I ever say I have not sinned, I make you a liar and I show that your Word is not within me. I choose to walk in the Spirit, that I will not fulfill the lusts of my flesh.

Scriptures: John 1:9; Romans 3:23; Romans 6:23; Galatians 2:20; Psalm 119:9; Psalm 119:11; 1 John 1:6-7; Romans 8:28-39; 1 John 1:10; Romans 8:1.

Personal Affirmation: "Let us lay aside every weight, and the sin which doth so easily beset us, and let us run with patience the race that is set before us, looking unto Jesus the author and finisher of our faith; who for the joy that was set before him endured the cross, despising the shame, and is set down at the right hand of the throne of God" (Hebrews 12:1-2).

Now that I'm free from sin, I choose to stand fast in the liberty wherewith Christ has set me free. (See Galatians 5:1.)

Reflection: *"God's Word will keep you from sin, but sin will keep you from God's Word"* (Billy Graham).

48

SKEPTICISM

He staggered not at the promise of God
through unbelief; but was strong in faith,
giving glory to God.

(Romans 4:20)

Central Focus: Skepticism is a form of doubt, and I now reject all doubt. I will stand upon God's promises, because I know all other ground is sinking sand.

Prayer: Dear heavenly Father, I thank you for the critical-thinking skills you've imparted to me, but I do not want those skills to lead me into realms of doubt or skepticism about you and your ways. Strengthen my faith, Lord God; strengthen me according to your Word. Lord, I believe, and I ask you to help me in all areas of unbelief.

I want to enter your rest, Lord God, and to stay there. I know that unbelief and skepticism will keep me from entering your rest. A heart of unbelief is an evil heart, and I want my heart to be pure, dear Father. Forgive me of all doubt and skepticism.

With your help and through your grace, I will labor to enter into your rest instead of falling into unbelief, for I know that your Word is quick and powerful and sharper than any two-edged sword. Thank you for revealing this truth to me, Father.

I believe your Word, Lord, and I believe that Jesus Christ is your precious Son. I love you, Father, and I will replace all skepticism with faith which will make me whole. Praise the Lord! I want to be full of faith and full of the Holy Ghost. Fill me afresh with your Spirit, Father.

Thank you for justifying me through faith. Thank you for the armor you've provided for me. I put on your armor now, Lord God, and I will be strong in you and in the power of your might. Above all, I take the shield of faith, wherewith I will be able to quench all the fiery darts of the wicked, including skepticism and doubt.

In Jesus' name I pray, Amen.

Scriptures: Psalm 119:28; Mark 9:24; Hebrews 3:11-12; Hebrews 4:11-12; Acts 8:37; Mark 10:52; Acts 11:24; Galatians 2:16; Ephesians 6:10-11; Ephesians 6:16.

Personal Affirmation: I am a believer, not a skeptic.

Reflection: *"Faith works love, works by love, and loves to work"* (Charles H. Spurgeon).

49

SUICIDAL TENDENCIES

I call heaven and earth to record this day
against you, that I have set before you life and
death, blessing and cursing: therefore choose
life, that both thou and thy seed may live: that
thou mayest love the Lord thy God, and that
thou mayest obey his voice, and thou mayest
cleave unto him: for he is thy life,
and the length of thy days.

(Deuteronomy 30:19-20)

Central Focus: Thoughts of suicide never come from God. Therefore, I will stand against all such thoughts and I will choose life.

Prayer: Thank you for reminding me that you have set life and death before me, Father. Through your grace, I now choose life, that I would continue to live and love you, my God. You are my Shepherd, Lord God, and because this is true, I know I shall never experience want or lack in my life. Thank you for restoring my soul and leading me beside the still waters and into the paths of righteousness for your name's sake. When I walk through the valley of the shadow of death, I will fear no evil, for you are with me and your rod and staff bring me comfort. Surely goodness and mercy will follow me and I will dwell in your house forever.

Thank you for restoring my soul, dear Lord, and delivering me from any thoughts of suicide. Show me the path of life, Father, for you are the strength of my life and with you is the fountain of life. Your loving-kindness is better than life to me.

Give me your wisdom, Lord, for I realize that your wisdom is a tree of life for me. I desire to walk in your wisdom and in your righteousness, for I realize that the way of life is found in your righteousness. Thank you for giving me abundant and eternal life, Lord.

By your mercies to me I present my body as a living sacrifice unto you, holy and acceptable unto you. I realize that this is my reasonable service to you, Father. Help me not to be conformed to this world, but to be transformed by the renewing of my mind, that I might prove what is your good, acceptable, and perfect will.

Thank you for delivering me from all thoughts of suicide.

Scriptures: Deuteronomy 30:19-20; Psalm 23; Psalm 16:11; Psalm 36:9; Psalm 63:3; Proverbs 3:18; Proverbs 10:16-17; John 10:10; John 3:16.

Personal Affirmation: Thoughts of suicide are from the devil. I renounce him now in the precious name of Jesus who has given life to me—abundant and eternal life.

Reflection: *"Never forget this wise warning: Never make a negative decision in a down time. This is only a phase you are going through. It will pass. When it is over, you'll be glad you hung in there!"* (Robert Schuller).

50

TALKATIVENESS

In the multitude of words there wanteth

not sin: But he that refraineth his lips is wise.

The tongue of the Just is as choice silver; the

heart of the wicked is Little worth.

The lips of the righteous feed many.

(Proverbs 10:19-21)

Central Focus: Self-control is an important key in learning to use my tongue in the ways God wants me to use it. I will allow the Holy Spirit within me to help me to control my tongue and to use the wonderful gift of speech in the best possible ways.

Prayer: Heavenly Father, thank you for the gift of speech. It truly is a wonderful gift. May the words of my mouth, the meditations of my heart, and the actions of my life be acceptable unto you. Help me to be less talkative, Father, and to become a better listener. I now realize that many words usually produce sin, and I never want to sin with my tongue.

Help me not ever to be prideful in speech, or to backbite with my tongue, and help me to keep my tongue from evil. Instead, I want my tongue to become the pen of a ready writer. My tongue shall speak of your Word, Father, and, as I do so, my tongue will be a source of health and blessing to myself and others.

Though my tongue is a little member, it can get involved in boasting great things. It can also cause a raging inferno. Father, I never want to use my tongue in destructive ways. Help me to tame my tongue, to use my tongue to bless you and others, and to keep my tongue pure.

Father, I love the life you've given to me. Help me to refrain my tongue from evil and keep me from ever speaking guile again. With your help, Lord God, I will not grieve the Holy Spirit ever again and I will get rid of all bitterness, wrath, anger, and evil speaking. Help me to be kind, tenderhearted, and forgiving toward others at all times.

Thank you for forgiving me of the abuse and misuse of my tongue, Father.

Scriptures: Psalm 19:14; Proverbs 10:19-21; Psalm 12:3; Psalm 15:3; Psalm 34:13; Psalm 45:15; Proverbs 12:18; James 3:5-11; 1 Peter 3:10; Ephesians 4:30-32.

Personal Affirmation: God has put a watch before my lips. I will use my tongue to praise Him, encourage others, pray, and to speak the truth in love. I will be swift to hear, slow to speak, and slow to wrath in my dealings with others. (See James 1:19.)

Reflection: *"Bernard [of Clairvaux] warns us that the spiteful tongue 'strikes a deadly blow at charity in all who hear him speak and, so far as it can, destroys root and branch, not only in the immediate hearers but also in all others to whom the slander, flying from lip to lip, is afterwards repeated.' Guarding the reputation of others is a deep and lasting service"* (Richard Foster).

51

TEMPER

A stone is heavy, and the sand weighty;
but a fool's wrath is heavier than them both.
wrath is cruel, and anger is outrageous.

(Proverbs 27:3-4)

Central Focus: Realizing that wrath and anger can never produce the righteousness of God (see James 1:20), I choose to forsake all anger and wrath. I want to walk in the righteousness of God.

Prayer: Father God, please forgive me for my hasty spirit, my anger, and my wrath. As I confess my sins to you, I know you are forgiving me and cleansing me from all unrighteousness. Thank you, Father.

Through your grace and with your help I will refrain from all anger from this time forward. Fill me afresh, dear Lord, with the Holy Spirit, that I might walk in self-control from this time forward. I want to control my temper at all times, Father.

Your Word speaks to me at all times, Father. It tells me, for example, that a wrathful person stirs up strife, but he who is slow to anger appeases strife. Help me to be slow to anger, Lord. From this time forward I will cease from anger and forsake all wrath. Your Word assures me, Father, that those who are slow to wrath have great understanding. I want to be an understanding person who is slow to wrath at all times.

Realizing that wrath is a work of the flesh, I will seek your power to overcome it, Lord. Through your grace I will mortify my flesh and put on the new man, which is renewed in knowledge after your image.

I'm so glad you have not appointed me to wrath, but you have appointed me to obtain salvation by the Lord Jesus Christ. I receive the gift of salvation through Him. Thank you, Father. Now I am a new person in Jesus Christ. Old things are passed away, and all things have become new to me. Hallelujah!

In the name of the Savior I pray, Amen.

Scriptures: 1 John 1:9; Galatians 5:23; Proverbs 15:18; Psalm 37:8; Proverbs 14:29; Colossians 3:5-10; 1 Thessalonians 5:9; James 1:20; 2 Corinthians 5:17.

Personal Affirmation: God is enabling me to control my temper. He will not fail me as I put all wrath and anger behind me.

Reflection: *"Real goodness does not attach itself merely to this life—it points to another world. Political or professional reputation cannot last forever, but a conscience void of offense before God and man is an inheritance for eternity"* (Daniel Webster).

52

TRIALS

That the trial of your faith, being much more precious than of gold that perisheth, though it be tried with fire, might be found unto praise and honour and glory at the appearing of Jesus Christ.

(1 Peter 1:7)

Central Focus: The trials of life help me to grow stronger. I thank God in everything, including the trials I am going through.

Prayer: Father God, thank you for this trial of my faith. It truly is more precious than that of gold which perishes. I want my response to this trial to be praise, honor, and glory at the appearing of Jesus Christ, whom having not seen, I love. Though I cannot see him, believing, I rejoice with unspeakable joy and full of glory, receiving the end of my faith, even the salvation of my soul. In everything, even this trial, I will give thanks, for I realize this is your will in Christ Jesus concerning me. Thank you, Father.

Dear Lord, I don't think it is strange that I am going through this trial. Instead, I rejoice in the midst of it, because I realize I am a partaker of Christ's sufferings, and what an honor that is for me. When His glory is revealed, I will be glad with exceeding joy.

Thank you for showing me that no temptation (or trial) has come to me but such as is common to all people. Thank you for your faithfulness, Father. I know you will not permit me to be tried beyond what I am able to face, but with each trial and temptation you will give me a way to escape, that I shall be able to endure it. Thank you for this promise, dear God.

Enduring this trial leads me into happiness, for I realize that when I am tried and if I endure unto the end, I shall receive the crown of life which you have promised to all who love you. I love you, Lord. I love you with all my heart.

Thank you for showing me that the trials of this life and the sufferings of this present time are nothing in comparison to the glory you will reveal. In all these things, Lord, I am more than a conqueror through my Lord Jesus Christ in whose name I pray.

Scriptures: 1 Peter 1:7-9; 1 Thessalonians 5:18; 1 Peter 4:12; 1 Corinthians 10:13; James 1:12; Romans 8:18; Romans 8:37.

Personal Affirmation: I refuse to become weak in face of the trials I am going through. God's strength is being made perfect in this situation. (See 2 Corinthians 12:9.)

Reflection: *"Faith faces everything that makes the world uncomfortable—pain, fear, loneliness, shame, death—and acts with a compassion by which these things are transformed, even exalted"* (Samuel H. Miller).

53

UNTHANKFULNESS

Rejoice evermore. Pray without ceasing. In
everything give thanks: for this is the will
of God in Christ Jesus concerning you.

(1 Thessalonians 5:16-18)

Central Focus: I must learn to count my blessings instead of focusing on my problems. Through God's grace I will become a truly thankful person.

Prayer: Heavenly Father, thank you. Thank you for everything. Thank you for life itself. Teach me how to be a person who always rejoices, prays without ceasing, and gives thanks in everything. I realize this is your will concerning me.

I will make a joyful noise unto you, O Lord, and come before your presence with thanksgiving, because I know who you are. Thank you for creating me; I am a sheep in your pasture. Therefore, I enter your gates with thanksgiving and I go into your courts with praise. I am so thankful to you, and I bless your holy name. You are so good to me, and your truth endures to all generations.

Great is your faithfulness, Father. Morning by morning new mercies I see. You have supplied all my needs according to your riches in glory by Christ Jesus. I can do all things through Him. Thank you so much for the power you've imparted to me.

Everything I know about you, Father, and everything I've experienced from your hands cause me to rejoice in you, and I will do so always from now on. Thanks be to you, Lord. Thank you for giving me the victory through my Lord Jesus Christ.

I will never be unthankful again, Lord. My life is full of blessings. Thank you so much for blessing me with all spiritual blessings in heavenly places in Christ. In His name I pray, Amen.

Scriptures: 1 Thessalonians 5:16-18; Psalm 100; Lamentations 3:23; Philippians 4:19; Philippians 4:13; Acts 1:8; Philippians 4:4; 1 Corinthians 15:57; Ephesians 1:3.

Personal Affirmation: My heart is filled with thanksgiving for who God is and all He has done in my life. I will never be unthankful again.

Reflection: *"Great is thy faithfulness! Great is thy faithfulness! Morning by morning new* *mercies I see; all I have needed thy hand has provided; great is thy faithfulness, Lord, unto me!"* (Thomas O. Chisholm).

54

WEAKNESS

My grace is sufficient for thee:

for my strength is

made perfect in weakness.

(2 Corinthians 12:9)

Central Focus: My weakness is an opportunity to show forth God's strength. Through His grace I will rise above my weakness and I will be strong in the Lord and in the power of His might.

Prayer: Lord God, you are my strength, and I can do all things through Christ who strengthens me. I choose to rise above my weakness and to walk in your strength. Thank you for your grace, which is sufficient for me and for your strength, which is made perfect in my weakness.

Without you I can do nothing, but through your strength I can accomplish all things. You are my light and my salvation, Lord, and you are the strength of my life. As I wait upon you, I am filled with courage because you are strengthening my heart. Thank you, Father.

I love you, O Lord, my strength. Thank you for girding me with strength. You are my strength and my shield. You are my strength in times of trouble. Father, you are my refuge and my strength, a very present help in times of trouble. Therefore, I will not fear nor be weak any longer. Thank you, Lord.

My soul will wait only upon you, Lord, for my expectation is from you. You are my rock and my salvation. You are my defense, and I shall not be moved. In you I have my salvation and my glory. You are the rock of my strength and my refuge. I will trust in you at all times and pour out my heart before you.

I will go forth in your strength, not in my own might or power, because I know that it's not by my might or power, but it is by your Spirit that I shall prevail. Thank you, Father.

Scriptures: Philippians 4:13; 2 Corinthians 12:9; John 15:5; Psalm 27:1; Psalm 18:1; Psalm 18:39; Psalm 28:7; Psalm 46:1-2; Psalm 62:5-8; Psalm 70:16; Zechariah 4:6.

Personal Affirmation: I am no longer weak or weary. Through faith I will mount up with wings as eagles, run and not be weary, and walk without fainting. (See Isaiah 40:31.)

Meditation: *"O Christ, let me move over and let Thee take the wheel, and then I'll get through this business of living without mishap. Amen"* (E. Stanley Jones).

CHAPTER FIVE

PRAYER PROMISES FROM GOD'S WORD

So shall my word be that goeth forth out of my mouth: It shall not return unto me void, but it shall accomplish That which I please, and it shall prosper in the thing whereto I sent it.

(Isaiah 55:11)

The following passages from both the Old and New Testaments reveal some of God's promises about prayer—what He promises to do in response to your prayers. This is not a complete list of the prayer promises, but each one reveals the heart of God to us.

Our Father wants us to pray even though He knows what we have need of before we express those needs to Him. (See Matthew 6:8.) Praying His Word involves so much more than simply saying a prayer, for it enables us to appropriate His promises while we pray.

Therefore, prayer is important for a variety of reasons:

- It helps us to get to know our heavenly Father better.

- It enables us to express our needs to Him.

- Through intercessory prayer, we are ministering to other people.

- Praying God's Word builds our faith.

- Prayer is a two-way conversation with God.

- Through prayer we learn to ascertain His voice speaking to us.

- Prayer helps us to focus on the things of God, those things that are eternal.

- Prayer leads us into worship and meditation.

- When we confess our sins through prayer, God is faithful and just to forgive us our sins. (See 1 John 1:9.)

- Through prayer we express our thanks to God.

- God meets our needs in response to our prayers.

These are just some of the things that happen when we pray. Each of these is strengthened and made more complete when we pray the Scriptures.

Now let's look at specific prayer promises to see what God promises to do when we pray.

For then shalt thou have thy delight in the Almighty, and shalt lift up they face unto God. Thou shalt make thy prayer unto him, and he shall hear thee. (Job 22:26-27)

Because he hath set his love upon me, therefore will I deliver him: I will set him on high, because he hath known my name. He shall call upon me, and I will answer him: I will be with him in trouble; I will deliver him, and honour him. With long life will I satisfy him, and shew him my salvation. (Psalm 91:14-16)

And it shall come to pass, that before they call, I will answer; and while they are yet speaking, I will hear. (Isaiah 65:24)

I will hasten my word to perform it. (Jeremiah 1:12)

Then shall ye call upon me, and ye shall go and pray unto me, and I will hearken unto you. (Jeremiah 29:12)

Call unto me, and I will answer thee, and shew thee great and mighty things, which thou knowest not. (Jeremiah 33:3)

But thou, when thou prayest, enter into thy closet, and when thou hast shut thy door, pray to thy Father which is in secret; and thy Father which seeth in secret shall reward thee openly. (Matthew 6:6)

Your Father knoweth what things ye have need of, before ye ask him. (Matthew 6:8)

Ask, and it shall be given you; seek, and ye shall find; knock, and it shall be opened unto you: for every one that asketh receiveth; and he that seeketh findeth; and to him that knocketh it shall be opened. (Matthew 7:7-8)

Verily I say unto you, Whatsoever ye shall bind on earth shall be bound in heaven: and whatsoever ye shall loose on earth shall be loosed in heaven. Again I say unto you, That if two of you shall agree on earth as touching any thing that they shall ask, it shall be done for them of my Father which is in heaven. For where two or three are gathered together in my name, there am I in the midst of them. (Matthew 18:18-20)

Verily I say unto you, If ye have faith, and doubt not, ye shall not only do this which is done to the fig tree, but also if ye shall say unto this mountain, Be thou removed, and be thou cast into the sea; it shall be done.

And all things, whatsoever ye shall ask in prayer, believing, ye shall receive. (Mathew 21:21-22)

And whatsoever ye shall ask in my name, that will I do, that the Father may be glorified in the Son. If ye shall ask any thing in my name, I will do it. (John 14:13-14)

If ye abide in me, and my words abide in you, ye shall ask what ye will, and it shall be done unto you. (John 15:7)

Verily, verily, I say unto you, whatsoever ye shall ask the Father in my name, he will give it you. Hitherto have ye asked nothing in my name: ask, and ye shall receive, that your joy may be full. (John 16:23-24)

Confess your faults one to another, and pray one for another, that ye may be healed. The effectual fervent prayer of a righteous man availeth much. (James 5:16)

And this is the confidence that we have in him, that, if we ask any thing according to his will, he heareth us: and if we know that he hear us, whatsoever we ask, we know that we have the petitions that we desired of him. (1 John 5:14-15)